THE CHOSEN CARETAKERS

THE CHOSEN CARETAKERS

Angel Marie's Story

SHURANDA HALL

Foreword by Iris A. Strachan

Contents

Acknowledgements vii
Dedication x

1	Foreword	1
2	Introduction	4
3	The Beginning	11
4	Long Suffering	22
5	Transition to Glory	41
6	Surrender	51
7	Grace	54
8	Rest	57
9	Trust	61
10	Gratitude	65
11	Death	70
12	Merely Caretakers	74
13	Higher Ways	81
14	Year 2023	83

Memories 89

Prayer of Salvation and Surrender 95

Acknowledgements

- To my heavenly father, Jesus Christ, who found me worthy of parenting His wonderful daughter. Thank you for lending Marie to us for six life-changing years and for the grace to prevail through some extremely tough times. Thank you for being my source of strength and my healer during my darkest moments.

- My husband, Alexander Hall, your unwavering support has been my anchor from the moment Marie entered our lives. I still cherish the words you whispered at her birth, reminding me that this was not a battle we had to face alone. While many marriages crumbled under such weight, we drew closer, fortified by God's grace. I am forever grateful for your love and strength.

- To my mother, Iris A. Strachan, your unwavering faith in God, even in the face of life's most daunting challenges, has been a beacon of strength for me. Your multifaceted support and guidance, especially during the creation of this book, have been invaluable. I am blessed to have you as my mother and editor. I love you dearly.

- To my spiritual parents, Apostle Emmanuel and Pastor Ibukun Adewusi, thank you for taking me in as your own. Apostle, your belief in me and your push for me to exceed my own expectations have been transformative. Thank you for holding me accountable and ensuring this book was released on time. Pastor Ibukun, your love and comfort have been my solace. When I doubted my ability to express my emotions on paper, you reassured me that my vulnerability would touch many hearts.

- To my children, Jayden, Sade, and Josiah Hall, thank you for always loving and supporting me, even during my burnout stage, when I may not have been the nicest mom. Thank you for all the love and care you gave Marie while she was with us. You all have experienced more than many other children would ever experience and had to assume responsibilities earlier than you probably should have. Your sacrifices have not gone unnoticed, and I pray that Jesus rewards you abundantly for them.

Scripture quotations marked NLT are taken from the Holy Bible, New Living Translation, Copyright © 1996, 2004, 2015 by Tyndale House Foundation. Used by permission of Tyndale House Publishers, Inc., Carol Stream, Illinois 60188. All rights reserved.

Scripture quotations marked NKJV are taken from the New King James Version®. Copyright © 1982 by Thomas Nelson. Used by permission. All rights reserved.

Scripture quotations from The Authorized (King James) Version. Rights in the Authorized Version in the United Kingdom are vested in the Crown. Reproduced by permission of the Crown's patentee, Cambridge University Press

Copyright © 2024 by Shuranda Hall

All rights reserved. No part of this book may be reproduced in any manner whatsoever without written permission except in the case of brief quotations embodied in critical articles and reviews.

First Printing, 2024

ISBN: 978-1-7777310-5-2 (paperback)
ISBN: 978-1-7777310-6-9 (e-book)

Published by: Shuranda Hall

For Angel Marie

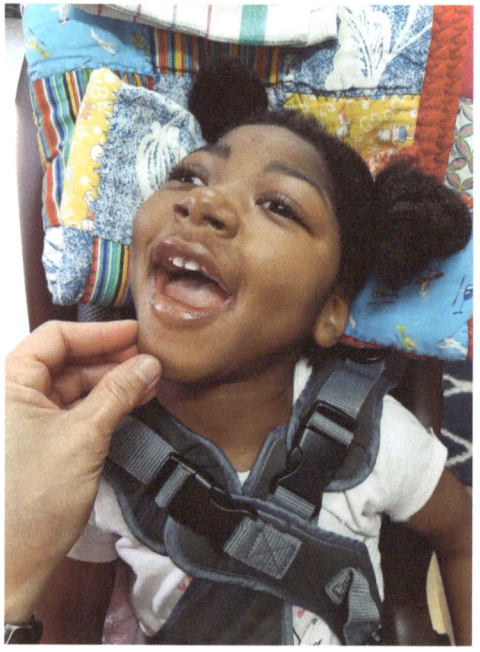

This book is dedicated to our angel, Marie.

Your presence has been a true blessing in our lives and you have inspired many. Though we miss you dearly, we find solace in knowing you are in a better place. We know that sickness was not your story, and death is not your end. As you enjoy your heavenly home, we will continue to share your beautiful story.

You are forever cherished, and your legacy lives on.

I

Foreword

"Ye have not chosen me, but I have chosen you, and ordained you, that ye should go and bring forth fruit, and that your fruit should remain: that whatsoever ye shall ask of the Father in my name, he may give it you."
John 15:16 KJV

One truth about the beginning of the scripture above is that God chose me, ordained me to be fruitful even amid an ongoing crisis...

When I read the book's title, I could not help but reflect on the birth of my firstborn daughter many years ago. After giving birth, I was taken to my room, and the nurse brought my baby girl to me. As I looked at her for the first time, my heart became full, and I thought, this is indeed a miracle; it is all God. With that revelation, I turned my face to the wall and silently wept; giving God praise and thanks for this miracle, I presented her back to God. I knew all too well that all the glory belonged to God.

Fast forward some years later, this baby girl will blossom into a beautiful woman of God, embrace the miracle of giving birth, and also the miracle of a "rainbow baby." As she writes her testimonies, it is evident that God is using every experience to shape her, mold her character and propel her into destiny- the path He desires. It is evident that Mrs. Hall, no doubt, has agreed with God that she is blessed to have been a "Chosen Caretaker" of God's prized possessions-children.

"Lo, children are an heritage of the LORD: And the fruit of the womb is his reward."
Psalm 127:3 KJV

Only with this understanding can we fully become the parents God intended us to be, fully instructing His children and training them in the ways of The Lord, even in the midst of calamities.

The blessing of a new healthy baby always brings joy to a family. No one envisions having a child with multiple birth defects. Trusting God goes beyond or surpasses the notion of waiting for God to show up in the time and in a specified way that we expect Him to. The omnipotent, omniscient, omnipresent God has carefully orchestrated the dynamics of your family. Number of children. Birthdates. Gender. God is The Creator. He makes the choices as He wills.

History shows that families may fall apart or bind closer when experiencing the loss of a child. Relying on self or the flesh can be physically and emotionally draining; however, having an authentic support system will definitely ensure that your restoration and transformation are perpetual. It is paramount that there is continual gathering with the saints, serving in ministry in the wake of adversity, as it takes the focus off of you. There must be a total reliance on Jesus Christ.

Trusting God in critical moments will always benefit your spiritual development. However, the reality is that sometimes it may become extremely difficult to hold on to a promise when it appears that what you are experiencing in the physical realm is heavy.

Facing the trauma and drama of the birth of her third child demanded every strand of faith in God.

"No mother wants to bury her child." These words capture the pain and agony experienced in the death of a six-year-old daughter. Shuranda writes about the traumatic and dramatic birth of her daughter and the challenges they encountered as a family. Through her testimonies, she was able to regain the faith that seemed to be absent at the onset of the trauma. In the midst of it all, renewing her mind to hold onto God and to "Cast all her cares upon Him..." brought balance back to her life.

As you read this book, you will engage in intimate conversations through the testimonies that provide you with opportunities to reflect on questions such as the value of life, facing the death of a child, serving and living while grieving. Is it possible? If you have ever questioned the parenting role, this book is for you. It will assist you in being the best parent according to God's divine order. As you hear the testimonies, you will be encouraged to examine your relationship with God and assess your confidence and faith. As a believer in Jesus Christ, it will provoke you to examine the evidence of the fruit of the spirit in your life, particularly when faced with a difficult situation. You will definitely examine and realign yourself to God's purpose for your parenthood and the assignment He has given. To be "The Chosen Caretaker", among other things, there must be an act of self-denial, a renewing of the mind, and a commitment to God's purpose. You are chosen.

Iris A. Strachan
(mother, confidant, teacher, and friend of the author)

2

Introduction

Testimony - Jan 2017

On Saturday, June 25th, 2016, I received surprising news: I was pregnant. With two young children and a tight budget, my husband and I were caught off guard. We hadn't planned for another baby, and we had taken precautions. However, recognizing children as blessings from God, we shifted our mindset from "Why now?" to "Wow, God thinks we're capable and worthy of another baby; He chose us." We quickly embraced the idea of adding to our family.

The following month, on Sunday, August 14th, I experienced some abnormal bleeding, prompting a visit to the Emergency room. After a lengthy wait and examination, I was discharged with advice to see my family physician the next day. Although the doctor didn't seem overly concerned, the bleeding worsened the next morning, Monday, August 15th, leading me back to the emergency room around 7 am. Further tests and an ultrasound revealed devastating news: I had suffered an "incomplete miscarriage." The fetus had stopped growing, there was no heartbeat, and my HCG levels had plummeted. I was warned to expect severe cramping and heavy bleeding as the miscarriage progressed.

This became the most physically painful experience of my life. Despite the pain, I pressed on with preparations for my son's fifth birthday party scheduled for that day. There was no way I could disappoint him.

I spoke to my pastors, who prayed fervently for complete healing, for the bleeding to cease, for the heartbeat to return, and for my HCG levels to normalize. However, God had other plans, and I ultimately lost the baby through a painful process. Initially, I felt hurt, sadness, and confusion. The first day after the miscarriage was particularly emotional for me. But to God's glory, I gradually began to feel better as time passed.

I had made a vow to trust God no matter what, to believe that His plan surpassed mine and that His ways were higher than mine. Despite not understanding the reasons behind the miscarriage, I remained at peace, confident that I would have another child someday. Little did I know that day would come sooner than expected.

A few weeks later, I started experiencing pregnancy symptoms again, which I attributed to my body regulating itself after the miscarriage. However, a home pregnancy test discounted my suspicions, and I was actually pregnant! This prompted a visit to the doctor for confirmation. An ultrasound revealed a sac, a baby, and a heartbeat. The doctor's response was one of surprise: "Wow, that was extremely quick!" They wanted to ensure there was actually a baby before starting the prenatal process.

Today, I am 24 weeks pregnant, eagerly anticipating the arrival of a baby girl in late Spring. I am grateful to God for almost immediately restoring what seemed lost or dead in the eyes of humans. His plans and timing are beyond our understanding. By trusting God in all circumstances, I have witnessed firsthand His ability to restore what appears to be dying or dead.

I gave birth to four children. Two girls and two boys. My youngest daughter died on July 13th, 2023, at the age of six. Now, I have three living children. Two boys and one girl. I still can't believe I just typed those words. This is actually my new reality. The child I spoke about in the previous testimony above, the "quick" miracle baby, is no longer here. That miscarriage is also no longer the most physically painful experience of my life. Have you ever experienced such emotional pain that you feel it physically? I did, with the loss of my daughter. The emotions were so strong that they began to manifest all over my body. I didn't understand. I still don't really understand, and I have so many questions. Many, many questions. Why didn't He heal my daughter on earth? Why save her at birth only to still let her die at the young age of six? Why did her life start with CPR and end with CPR? Why choose us to be her caretakers? What was the point of my faith? Did our faith not work? Would things have been different if we made more declarations? Ok, where did we really miss the mark? What was the point of all the struggle and holding faith all these years if she wasn't healed on Earth? If He had healed her, He would get the glory, wouldn't He? That was what was supposed to happen, right? God was supposed to heal my daughter from every ailment, and then He would get all the glory. It's perfect math. A perfect equation. There is a challenge, and God fixes the challenge. Everyone is wowed, and then they all give their lives to Christ. That's how this was meant to play out. It only makes perfect sense. That is what should have happened. At least to me, that's the only way this scenario would end properly.

Clearly, God had other plans - plans that I truly do not understand. I sometimes wonder if I ever will.

The Bible does say that His plans are way higher than our plans.

"For my thoughts are not your thoughts, neither are your ways my ways, saith the LORD. 9 For as the heavens are higher than the earth, so are my ways higher than your ways, and my thoughts than your thoughts." **Isaiah 55:8**

The truth is, I don't have to understand God's plans. I don't even have to agree. I really don't have a say at all. It all started when I decided to give my life to Jesus. I surrendered my life to Him, gave it away, and told Him He could use it how He pleased. What I am choosing to trust, though, is that my baby girl fulfilled her purpose and touched many lives. The one thing that many of us are striving to do is fulfill our purpose and touch many lives when doing so.

I have always loved dancing and was privileged to lead the dance ministry in my family church for a short time back in The Bahamas. When we relocated to Canada, we joined Cornerstone Christian Church of God, Edmonton. We regularly host Evangelistic programs called "Come and See". At our very first one in April 2015, I had the privilege to minister in dance to Tasha Cobbs's song "For Your Glory". Whew! If only I knew what I was publicly saying and declaring at that time. The beginning part of the song goes like this:

> "Lord, if I Find favour in Your sight
> Lord, please Hear my hearts cry
> I'm desperately waiting, To be where You are
> I'll cross the hottest desert, I'll travel near or far
> For Your glory, I will do anything
> Just to see You; To behold You as my King"

Do you guys really understand what those words are saying? The average temperature of the hottest desert hovers between 29 and 35 degrees Celsius, often exceeding 43 degrees Celsius during midday. They are not only hot but very dry and sunny. So here I am telling my Jesus that I will cross this blistering landmass (oh, and to put it into more perspective, the Sahara desert is 9,200,000 square kilometres) JUST for His Glory. I'm not saying any of this out of regret at all; rather, I want to emphasize that giving our lives to Christ means giving up our free will. He gave us freedom of choice, yet we say, "Father, thank you, but I give my life back to you; I trust you with it. I want what you want and will do what you want me to do. I will trust you even when things don't exactly go the way that I expect." So when I'm in the desert stage of life, and the wind is blowing sand in my eyes, and I can't see where I am going, Father, I will trust you. Your word says that you will be with us when we go through the fire and the flood, so Father, I will trust you. One of the hardest realities however, is when the end doesn't happen the way that you envisioned. I've learnt now, though, that if it's not a victorious ending, it's not yet the ending; it's just a part of the story.

Through it all, deciding to live for Jesus is still the best decision that I have ever made. As challenging as life has been, I can only imagine the excessive amount of turmoil, trauma, and mental health challenges that would have developed doing life without Jesus. Challenges are going to come regardless; it's much better to go through them with Jesus. He can be trusted. He may not always get the glory the way we want or think He should, but He will get it.

Sooner or later, you realize that the plan you orchestrated in your brain is far from what God has in mind. And that's ok. Though it hurts sometimes, though many questions still remain, though the child that I carried and birthed is no longer with us, though her body is buried at the cemetery, I sit back and trust Him. It's a decision I made: A decision to trust Him, even when it feels like He is nowhere to be found, especially when it feels like He is nowhere to be found. Yet, I will trust Him!

3

The Beginning

Let me backtrack a little bit. On May 13th, 2017, our family was blessed with a beautiful baby girl. As the previous testimony mentioned, Marie was a miracle baby. I had just miscarried a few weeks back, and the timing of when she was conceived really didn't make logical sense; it was a pure miracle.

I was so grateful to God for restoring that pregnancy so swiftly. It was perfect! Done in the way that only He can. Though a beautiful pregnancy and obviously God-sent, Marie's birth story wasn't actually glamorous; in fact, it was extremely dramatic and traumatic. My husband and I were going on our last date before she was due to come. I got all dressed up because I knew from experience that when my baby girl landed, life would definitely change, and date nights may look different for quite a while. We needed to take advantage of the free time before it was gone. We went to dinner at a fancy restaurant downtown. It had been on our bucket list for quite some time. Unexpectedly, while at dinner, I started experiencing very, very sharp pains in my abdomen. They were excruciating! I somehow knew in my heart that she was coming that night.

I hadn't experienced contractions before, as my previous births were all C-sections. As the pain increased, I thought that I was having extremely painful contractions, but I had nothing to compare them to. I would later discover that these pains were not contractions. In fact, they were way worse. I was having a placental abruption (basically, the uterus was tearing itself away from my body), and my sweet baby girl was losing oxygen. Every second mattered, and every second that passed could determine if there would be any brain damage or not. Of course, I didn't know any of this at the time. I just knew I was in lots of pain. We rushed to the hospital, and I was prepped for an emergency C-section. I was being poked and prodded in all directions. While one nurse was drawing my blood, another was inserting an IV in my other arm, and yet another nurse was inserting a catheter. My husband basically got pushed to the side and just had to wait. He was not allowed in the operating room for this delivery. He had been right by my side for the previous kids, but this time, due to the complications, it was me, Jesus and the medical team. It was eerily quiet during this surgery. I was used to the medical team talking about random topics, checking in on me, and making me laugh. But this time, it was so very quiet. I remember after what felt like days, one of the nurses came to me and said, "Your baby was a bit pale when she came out, but she is looking much better now." I said, "OK". I really had no idea what she was really saying. But I would find out soon enough.

So, picture this: when Marie made her grand entrance into the world, she wasn't exactly kicking and screaming like most babies do. Nope! She was still, and turning a shade of blue that made everyone in the room panic. The nurse had tried to explain to me what was going on, but I didn't understand at that moment. Apparently, "pale" meant blue, and blue meant Marie wasn't getting enough oxygen. It was touch and go for about eight agonizing minutes as the medical team fought to bring her back to life. They were just about to throw in the towel and call it quits, labelling her birth as a stillbirth. But then, on cue, divine intervention! God stepped in and breathed His breath of life once more. The resuscitation methods proved successful, and Marie took a deep breath on her own, proving once again that miracles do happen.

And so, the journey began! And let me tell you, it was a marathon, not a sprint. The first time I laid eyes on Marie, she was in an incubator. Holding her was out of the question. Shortly after the delivery, she had to be transported to the Royal Alexandra Hospital for specialized care. But before they took her, they wheeled her into my room for a quick peek. All I could do was gaze at her through the incubator window; they did let me sneak in a touch of her tiny hand.

I felt completely defeated. I was totally crushed. My whole vision of motherhood and birthing felt like it was slipping through my fingers once again. I'd never experienced that miraculous moment of holding my babies immediately after they were born. That initial skin-to-skin bonding was just a distant dream for me. And having my little ones in the same room as me after giving birth? Forget about it. Both my older kids got whisked off to the NICU straight after delivery. And now, here we go again with Marie, off to the NICU, this time in a whole different hospital. I mean, seriously?

Shortly after, I found myself in the same situation as Marie, needing to be transported to the Royal Alec. Unfortunately, I was still dealing with internal bleeding that showed no signs of abating. Despite efforts to control it, the situation remained critical. The medical team determined that my best chance for proper care was at the Alec, which was equipped for high-risk and emergency scenarios. So, off I went, following Marie's path to the next stage of our journey.

Marie was born on a Saturday night. I was privileged to see her on Monday morning after the medical team felt confident enough that the bleeding had stopped, and I believed that I was well enough to be out of bed. This was the moment I finally got to sit with my precious baby girl. But let me tell you, it was a sight that broke my heart into a million pieces. There she was, surrounded by what seemed like a mountain of machines and tubes. I mean, seriously, how could someone so tiny need all that stuff? The doctors weren't even sure if she'd make it through the night. She was hooked up to a ventilator, nutrition bags, antibiotics, seizure meds—you name it, she probably had it attached to her. She'd been through multi-organ failure and severe brain damage. It was devastating to see her lying there, so fragile and helpless. I wasn't even allowed to hold her properly; just barely managed to touch her. She looked so lifeless, and it tore me apart inside. I cried until there were no tears left.

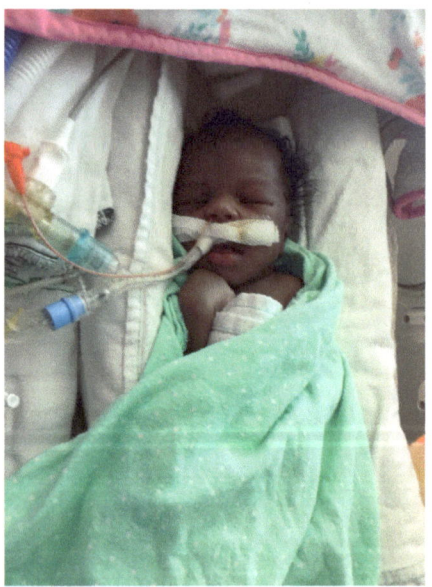

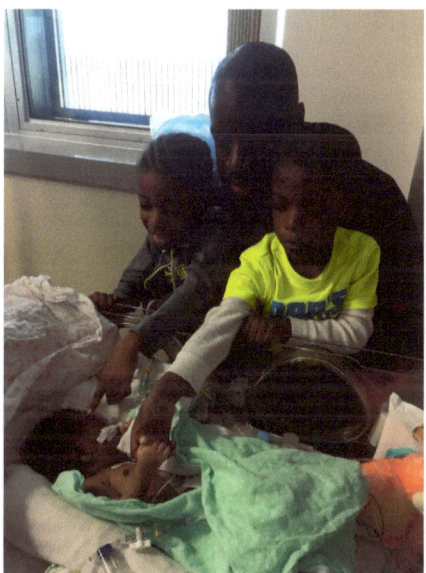

In my past visits to the NICU with my older son and daughter, I'd pass by the really critical babies on my way to see my own. But this time, there was no getting around it—my baby girl was the critical one, fighting for her life. There was no walking past that reality.

Leaving Marie's bedside that first visit, I was a wreck—completely shaken and confused. But as I made my way out, I heard it loud and clear: "**Corinthians 2:5**". I was unfamiliar with this scripture, so I knew I had to look this one up. Unsure if it was 1 Corinthians or 2 Corinthians, I decided to check both. And as soon as I flipped to 1 Corinthians, it hit me like a ton of bricks. There it was: *"I did this so you would trust not in human wisdom but in the power of God."* (NLT version). Those words became my lifeline in the days, weeks, months, and years that followed. I clung to the belief that God's power would outshine every grim prognosis the doctors threw our way. That verse reminded me not to put all my faith in human knowledge but in God. I was convinced that God would use His power to heal Marie's brain and give her a fresh start. All I wanted was to see her walk, talk, and hear her say "Mommy." That thought kept me going through endless nights, countless doctor visits, and what felt like an eternity in the hospital. But as it turned out, reality had a different plan in store for us.

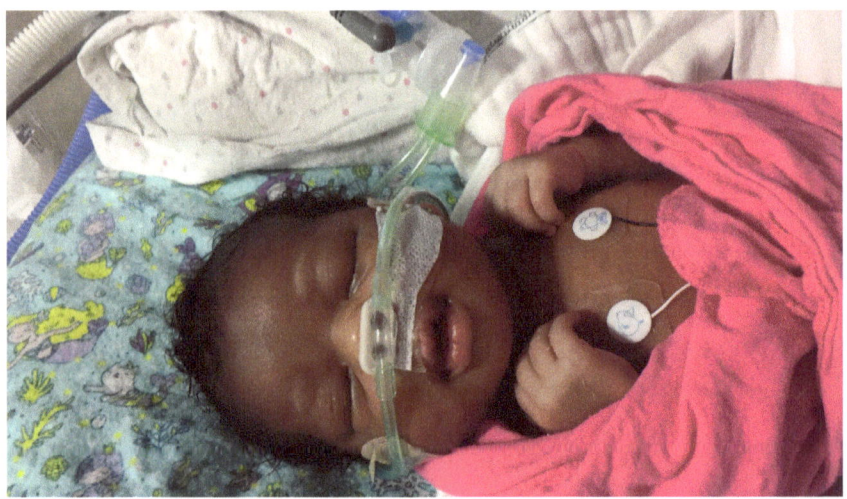

As I mentioned, my first two children had spent time in the NICU, but now this was different. There were never any major concerns or life-threatening reasons for them to be in the hospital. Jayden was born prematurely at 33 weeks but was pretty much being monitored for growth and feeding as he had to meet a certain weight to leave the hospital. He spent one month in the NICU. Sade, on the other hand, spent five days in the NICU. She was born full term, but her weight was considered smaller, and she experienced a bit of a challenge with her lungs initially. But Marie's situation was different. It was so complicated. There were so many things unknown. The MRI showed extreme brain damage. The doctors were unsure of what this even meant, leaving us unsure of what it meant. In the words of one of the nurses: "She is a very, very sick little girl."

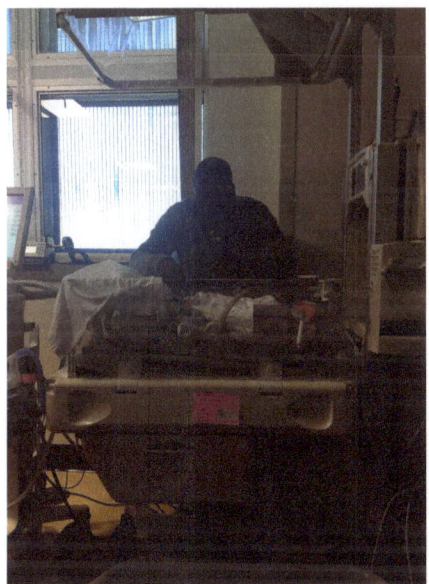

The only thing we had to hold on to was our faith. Literally nothing else. There weren't great expectations for Marie's life. In fact, there really wasn't any. It felt like everyone was waiting to see what would happen. How long would she last? How will she turn out? I remember a nurse actually saying to me, "She will probably never suck" when questions about bottle feeding were asked. The head physician said that he couldn't tell what the disability would be but that he knew there was definitely going to be a disability and developmental delay. There were so many meetings and plans for the negative possibilities and expectations. He even brought up conversations about pulling the plug or not resuscitating if there was a need to. I remember him asking if we had ever taken care of someone with a disability. He didn't think it was worth it to save her life if, for some reason, she started to slip away.

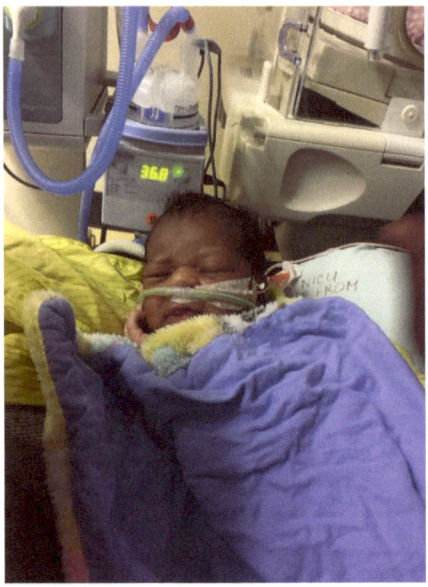

At this time, we were thinking, "What is this guy's problem?". Why is this even a discussion? God is going to heal her. And we began to activate our faith. To be honest with you, my faith was not an equal match for the doctor's reports and expectations at that time. In fact, I don't know if I can even say that I had faith. I was riding the faith of my husband, mother, and pastors. Everything felt so devastating. It was all so wrong. This was supposed to be my first baby that didn't have to go in the NICU, and now here we are again, in another country, and in a much worse situation with no answers and no positive projections. There is no way or words to explain the emotions that I felt during this time. This was the beginning of many doctor's visits, homecare visits, therapy sessions, sleepless nights, faith muscle-building… It was truly the definition of long-suffering… but as difficult as it may have been for us as her caretakers, imagine what she must have been experiencing.

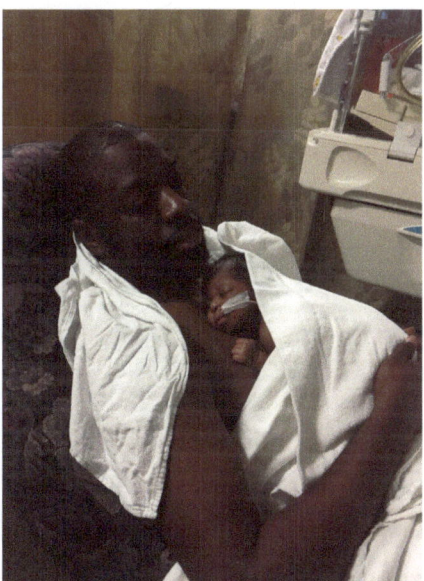

When the doctor who performed the Cesarean called to check on me, she said that when she cut me open and saw my insides, she thought to herself by the look of things that I should have been screaming down the hall as I came in. Her words were, "You did not appear to be in the pain that your body showed you were in." Apparently, after making the surgical incision, they (the medical team) found that blood was everywhere. I believe God protected me from experiencing that level of torture.

During a placental abruption of the uterus, the placenta tears away from the uterus, causing the baby to lose oxygen and nutrition. It is very uncommon and often results in premature delivery, loss of oxygen to the baby's brain, and, in extreme situations, stillbirth. I experienced internal bleeding, trapping the blood between the uterus and the placenta. I required blood transfusions and platelets in order to replenish the blood that was lost. Medication was given in an attempt to stop the bleeding, but it continued for some time. I remember being told that staples were used to close the incision instead of stitches in case the cut had to be opened up again. Often, in such extreme situations, either mom, baby, or both can die. This was not a joke; this was not a bad dream. It was reality; it was serious, and we had no idea what the next few years were actually going to consist of. And as much pain as I was in then, I will never know exactly how much pain Marie experienced during her time on earth as she was not able to communicate it with us. But, to the glory of God, we were both alive and "where there is life, there is hope."

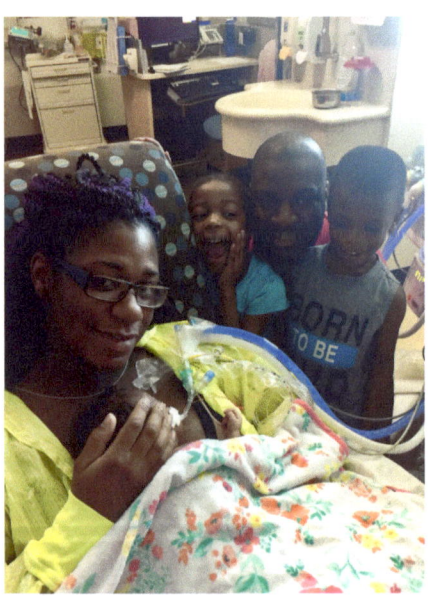

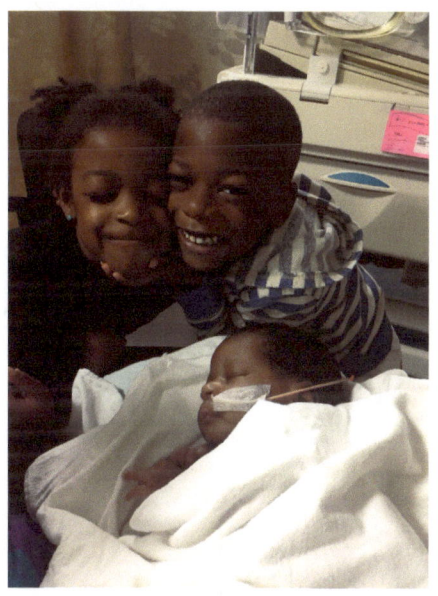

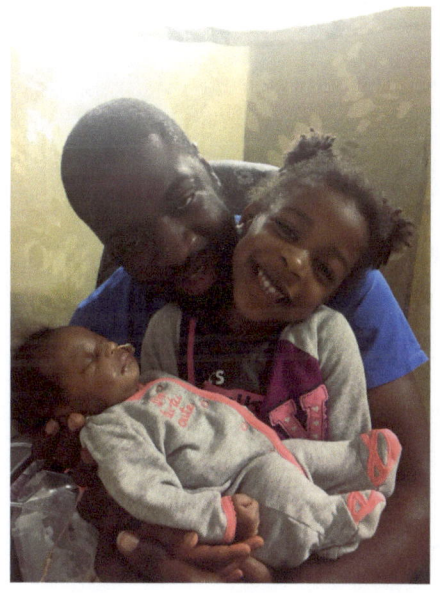

4

Long Suffering

Testimony - May 2022

I want to share my annual May testimony and express my gratitude to God for yet another year of preserving my life. Five years ago, both my daughter and I faced life-threatening complications during childbirth. But to the glory of God, we are still here today. I join in celebrating with all families who have experienced near misses during pregnancy and childbirth, and I am especially grateful for those close to me who were rescued by God from what could have been tragic situations.

I am thankful because my youngest daughter celebrated her fifth birthday on May 13th. Considering the uncertainty surrounding her survival during her first night, followed by a month-long hospital stay and years of medical interventions, her milestone birthday is truly a testament to God's faithfulness. His promises are indeed yes and Amen.

I also thank God for the village He has provided for us. Although my daughter couldn't spend her birthday with us, she enjoyed a memorable vacation in the Bahamas surrounded by family and friends who genuinely care for her. Their love and support have been invaluable throughout our journey.

There were countless trips to various doctors for Marie's care. From neurologists to pediatricians, physiotherapists to occupational therapists, and speech-language pathologists to developmental assistants, the list seemed endless. Even routine appointments like dental checkups and passport photos became major undertakings. I distinctly remember the hassle of planning for travel in 2019. Getting Marie's passport photos taken was no easy feat given her physical condition and the strict specifications required. We had to find creative ways to support her head without showing our hands, all while coaxing her to look at the camera and keep her mouth closed – tasks that were easier said than done. What should have been a quick ten-minute process for most families turned into an hour-long ordeal for us.

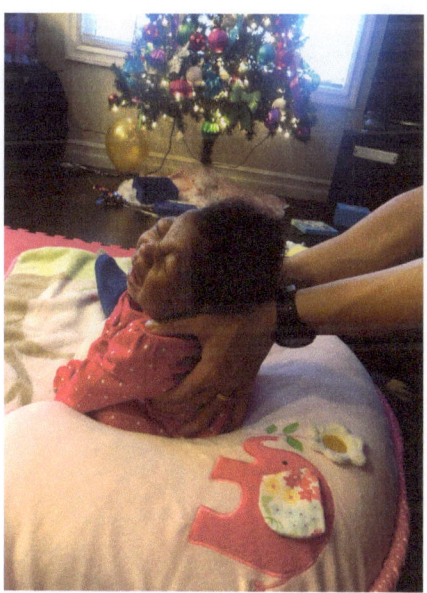

Dentist visits were another challenge altogether. Holding Marie down on our chests as she squirmed to break free was quite the workout. Since she couldn't follow the dentist's instructions to open and close her mouth, we had to insert a foam device and adjust it throughout the session as needed. It was quite the balancing act. We were informed that her next visit would likely require anesthesia in the operating room, which seemed absurd for routine teeth cleaning. However, she never did have that next dental visit.

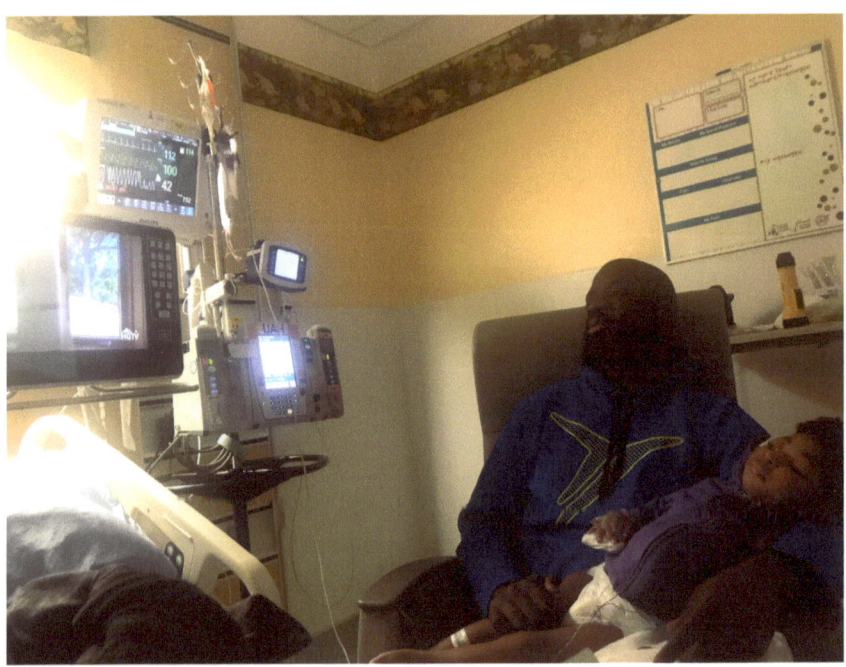

For our family, everything just seemed to require a little extra effort, planning, and patience. From feeding to bath time, car rides to family outings, and even bedtime routines – every aspect of our daily life looked different with Marie. She struggled with sleep apnea, gas, and muscle tension, rarely ever sleeping through the night. My own sleep was constantly interrupted, fragmented into short bursts of rest. Marie would sleep for a few hours at a time, sometimes even just 30 minutes, unable to shift her body while in bed like most people do naturally. Without that ability, she'd often wake crying, needing us to figure out what she needed – whether it was food, a diaper change, or just repositioning.

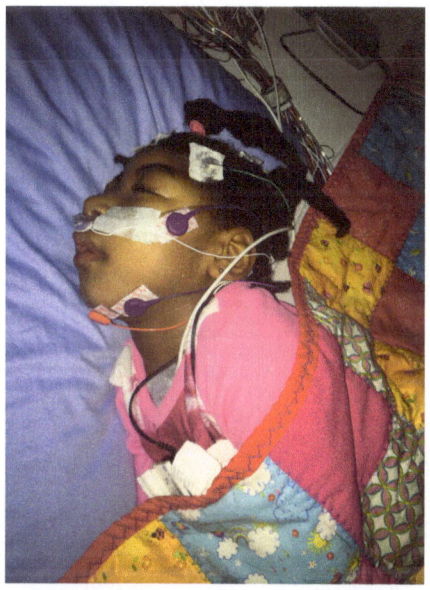

This disrupted sleep pattern took a toll on all of us, especially me. I often felt like a zombie in the mornings, struggling to function like a responsible adult. But somehow, we managed to push through. We banded together as a family, doing our best to maintain some sense of normalcy for our other children.

Despite the challenges, we were incredibly grateful that Marie was still with us. Every day felt like a victory, knowing that she had made it through another night. We clung to verses like **Ecclesiastes 9:4 NLT**, *"There is hope only for the living. As they say, 'It's better to be a live dog than a dead lion!"*, finding hope in the fact that she was still alive. We reminded ourselves of God's promises of healing and the assurance that all things work together for good for those who love Him (**Romans 8:28**). We held firmly onto the first word that God sent to me at her birth, *"I did this so you would trust not in human wisdom but in the power of God"* **1 Corinthians 2:5 NLT**. Even when circumstances seemed bleak, we held onto our faith, trusting in the power of God to see us through.

Long-suffering took on a whole new meaning for us during this time. It wasn't caused by other people, but the challenges we faced felt incredibly daunting. Year after year, we persevered through the trials, holding onto our faith even when it felt like nothing was going our way.

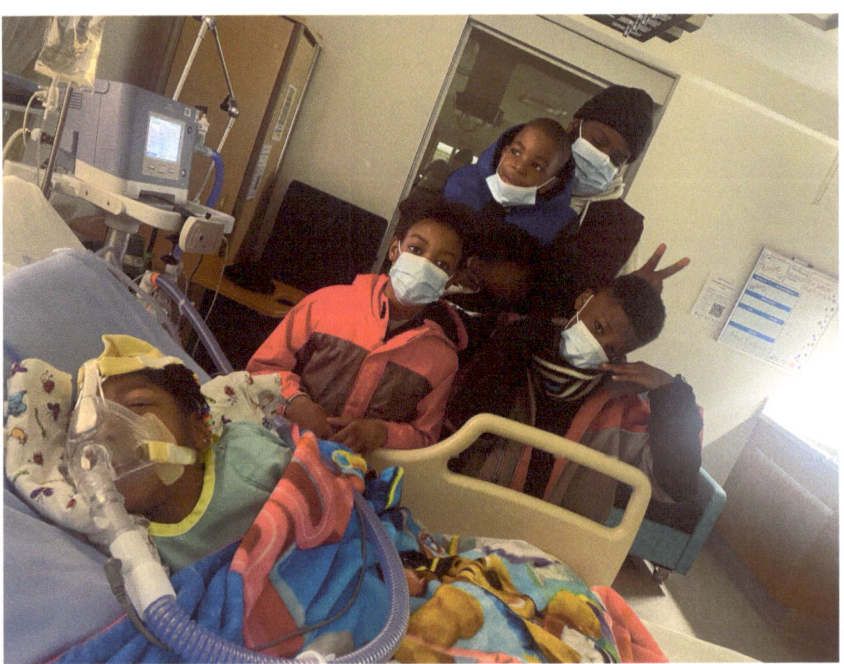

When we reflect on the concept of long-suffering in the Bible, several familiar names stand out: Joseph, Abraham and Sarah, Job, Moses and the Israelites, the woman with the issue of blood, Paul, David, and many more. Each of these individuals endured immense trials and tribulations, demonstrating remarkable patience and perseverance in the face of adversity.

Take Job, for example. Despite experiencing unimaginable suffering and loss, he remained steadfast in his faith, ultimately finding restoration and experiencing blessings even greater than before.

These stories serve as powerful reminders that, although the journey may be difficult and fraught with challenges, there is always hope for restoration and redemption. Through their examples, we are encouraged to endure with patience and trust in God's ultimate plan for our lives.

When Job prayed for his friends, the Lord restored his fortunes. In fact, the Lord gave him twice as much as before! Then, all his brothers, sisters, and former friends came and feasted with him in his home. And they consoled him and comforted him because of all the trials the Lord had brought against him. And each of them brought him a gift of money and a gold ring. So the Lord blessed Job in the second half of his life even more than in the beginning. For now he had 14,000 sheep, 6,000 camels, 1,000 teams of oxen, and 1,000 female donkeys. He also gave Job seven more sons and three more daughters. He named his first daughter Jemimah, the second Keziah, and the third Keren-happuch. In all the land no women were as lovely as the daughters of Job. And their father put them into his will along with their brothers.

Job lived 140 years after that, living to see four generations of his children and grandchildren. Then he died, an old man who had lived a long, full life. **Job 42:10-16 NLT**

Indeed, Joseph's story is a remarkable testament to God's faithfulness and the power of perseverance. Despite being sold into slavery by his own brothers and enduring unjust imprisonment, Joseph remained faithful to God. Through a series of divine interventions and his unwavering trust in God, Joseph eventually rose from the depths of despair to become the second-in-command to Pharaoh, ruler over all of Egypt.

His journey from the prison to the palace serves as a powerful reminder that God can turn even the most challenging circumstances into blessings beyond imagination. Joseph's story inspires us to trust in

God's providence and remain steadfast in our faith, knowing that He is always working for our good, even in the midst of adversity.

'Pharaoh said to Joseph, "I hereby put you in charge of the entire land of Egypt." Then Pharaoh removed his signet ring from his hand and placed it on Joseph's finger. He dressed him in fine linen clothing and hung a gold chain around his neck. Then he had Joseph ride in the chariot reserved for his second-in-command. And wherever Joseph went, the command was shouted, "Kneel down!" So Pharaoh put Joseph in charge of all Egypt. And Pharaoh said to him, "I am Pharaoh, but no one will lift a hand or foot in the entire land of Egypt without your approval." Then Pharaoh gave Joseph a new Egyptian name, Zaphenath-paneah. He also gave him a wife, whose name was Asenath. She was the daughter of Potiphera, the priest of On. So Joseph took charge of the entire land of Egypt. He was thirty years old when he began serving in the court of Pharaoh, the king of Egypt. And when Joseph left Pharaoh's presence, he inspected the entire land of Egypt.' **Genesis 41:41-46 NLT**

The woman who suffered from a prolonged issue of bleeding experienced complete healing when she reached out and touched the cloak of Jesus. In that moment, her years of suffering and despair were transformed into joy and relief. Not only was she physically healed, but she also received the blessing of Jesus' affirmation and peace. Her story serves as a powerful testament to the miraculous healing and transformative power of faith in Jesus Christ.

'A woman in the crowd had suffered for twelve years with constant bleeding. She had suffered a great deal from many doctors, and over the years she had spent everything she had to pay them, but she had gotten no better. In fact, she had gotten worse. She had heard about Jesus, so she came up behind him through the crowd and touched his robe. For she thought to herself, "If I can just touch his robe, I will be healed." Immediately the bleeding stopped, and she could feel in her body that she had been healed of her terrible condition. Jesus realized at once that healing power had gone out from him, so he turned around in the crowd and asked, "Who touched my robe?" His disciples

said to him, "Look at this crowd pressing around you. How can you ask, 'Who touched me?'" But he kept on looking around to see who had done it. Then the frightened woman, trembling at the realization of what had happened to her, came and fell to her knees in front of him and told him what she had done. And he said to her, "Daughter, your faith has made you well. Go in peace. Your suffering is over."' **Mark 5:25-34 NLT**

So, what happens when your prayers don't get answered the way you hoped? What do you do when the Lord doesn't swoop in and fix things the way you imagined? And what about when you're using scripture to pray and declare, but things still don't turn out the way the Bible says they should? I've been wrestling with these questions myself. But here's what I'm starting to realize: if things don't end in victory, it's more than likely not the end of the story. It's just another chapter, another twist in the plot.

Maybe we need to rethink what "the end" really means, especially in God's "playbook". After all, His idea of an ending might look a whole lot different than ours. The real "end" is when God gets all the glory. That's what He's all about—showcasing His power and goodness for all to see. Sometimes, that means He might delay or tweak the outcome we've been praying for if it means He'll get even more glory in the end. And hey, let's be real, it's not always a walk in the park when we're facing challenges.

Take Abraham and Sarah, for example. Waiting around for a child probably wasn't the highlight of their lives, but in the end, God proved Himself faithful by fulfilling His promises. And let's not forget about Job. Losing everything he held dear must have been beyond devastating. But God didn't leave him hanging; He stepped in as the ultimate restorer. So yeah, when it comes down to it, the endgame is all about God's glory, even if the journey isn't always smooth sailing.

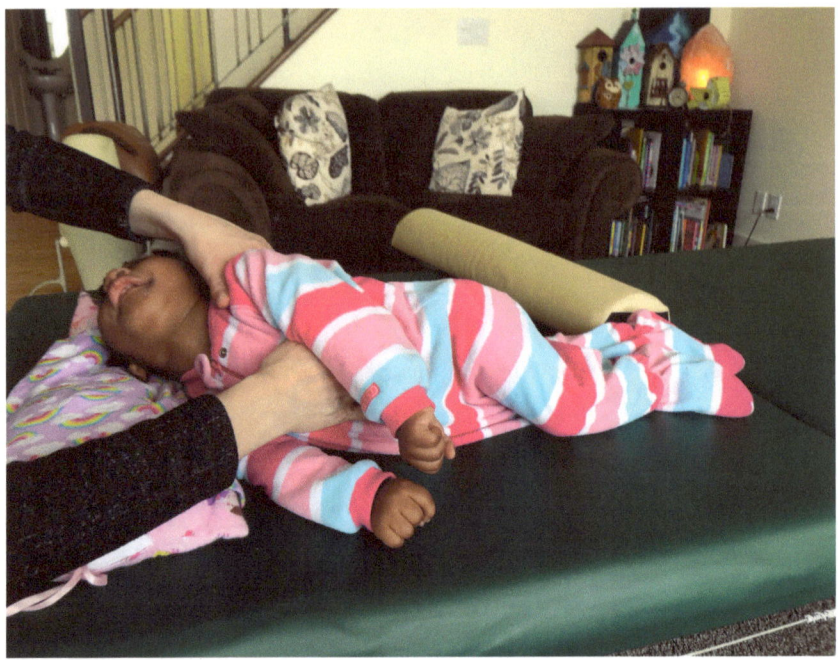

There were plenty of moments in Marie's journey that were downright tough to swallow. From one negative report after another to watching her life seemingly follow the path the medical reports laid out, it was like a punch in the gut. And you know what? I admit that it wasn't all sunshine and rainbows. But here's the thing: even in the midst of all that darkness, God showed up for me in ways I couldn't have imagined. He's been my rock, my constant help. His grace and faithfulness have been my lifeline through it all. And you know what else? He's been Marie's healer, too, just not in the way we expected. Instead of healing her here on earth, He chose to give her the ultimate healing by bringing her home to Him. And while my heart aches with the loss, I find solace in knowing she's in His loving arms, where pain and suffering have no place.

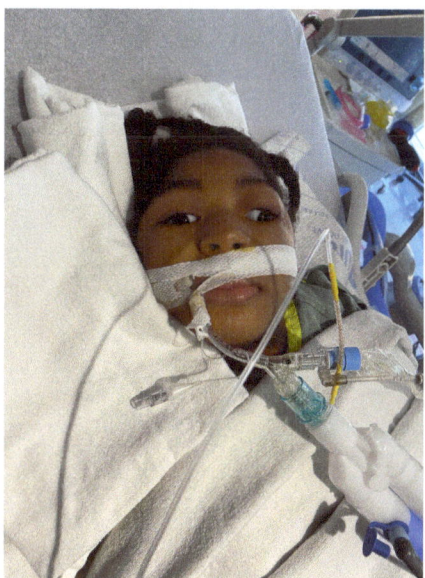

It's incredible how God works, isn't it? In the midst of all this pain and loss, He's busy healing not just our hearts but our minds, bodies, and so much more. There will be some challenges along the way in regard to parenting - whether it is behavioural, academic, emotional, you name it. But adopting the mindset of "God, I'll do anything for your glory" will help us as parents make the right calls, even if it means enduring some serious hardship. See, many folks end up inadvertently steering their kids away from their destinies because they can't handle the suffering that comes with it. But caring for Marie was a whole different ball game. It was intense, no doubt about it. But, If we had to do it all over again, we'd jump in with both feet, challenges and all, without hesitation.

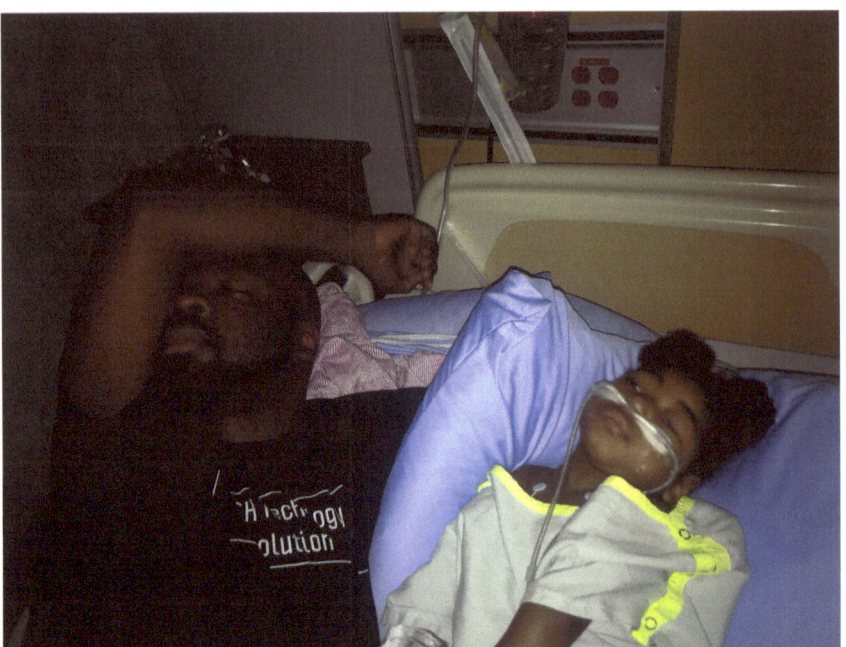

Testimony: January 2020

For an extended period, starting shortly after birth, Marie experienced feeding issues. She often refused to eat and would frequently bring up whatever little food she managed to swallow. Some days, she would vomit at least once every other day and sometimes multiple times daily. As her mother, I felt an immense responsibility to ensure she received the necessary nutrients, and dealing with this problem became extremely stressful for me.

On Christmas Day last year, Marie vomited twice, pushing me to the brink of breaking point. Feeling overwhelmed, I turned to God and sought guidance on who to reach out to for support. Through divine intervention, I connected with someone who shared their own testimony with me, offering valuable insight and revelation. It was during this conversation that I experienced a profound shift—I was finally able to surrender the situation entirely to God and let go of my need to control it.

Since then, I've been allowing God to lead me in how and when to feed Marie. Remarkably, Christmas Day 2019 marked the last time she vomited, and by God's grace, it will remain the last time. Not only has she stopped vomiting, but she has also been eating much more than ever before. This transformation is a testament to God's power to turn even the most persistent situations around when we place our trust in Him.

I am thankful to God for his healing, guidance, and perfect direction. I am also grateful for the testimonies of others and for friends who are walking in alignment with God's will, providing support and encouragement along the way.

You know, I've come to realize something about enduring through tough times—it's not always a one-and-done deal. Sometimes, when you think you've reached the light at the end of the tunnel, another challenge rears its head. Take Marie's situation, for instance. Just when we thought we had a handle on things, the vomiting started up again, and before we knew it, she was undergoing surgery for a G-tube (a tube that would allow her to be fed directly through her stomach). I felt like I had failed as a parent. How could I not figure out how to feed my own child? It was a devastating blow. While everyone else in the house was chowing down on meals, Marie was stuck being fed through a tube. But you know what? It was during these rough patches that the Lord helped me to begin shifting my perspective. Instead of focusing on the negative—what she "had to" go through—I started looking for the silver lining. Sure, she had to be fed through a tube, but I began to see it as a blessing that she had a way to get the nutrition she needed despite the feeding challenges. It was a mindset shift that was crucial for avoiding falling into a pit of complaints day in and day out. Sure, there were times when I was tired and couldn't help but grumble, but I soon realized that complaining only drained me even more. As I leaned more on God's grace, I found that the things that used to send me spiralling weren't as overwhelming anymore. His strength got me through one challenging situation at a time.

Testimony - Jan 2023

I want to express my gratitude to God for the miraculous healing of my 5-year-old daughter. In December, she fell ill with a respiratory virus that progressed to pneumonia. To the glory of God, she is now well and back home. However, this testimony goes beyond her healing—it's about the grace that sustained us during this challenging time.

On Monday, December 12th, she began struggling to breathe and experienced severe coughing fits. We rushed her to the Stollery Hospital, where she was promptly taken to the back for urgent care. About ten medical professionals tended to her, and there was even discussion of intubation due to the severity of her breathing difficulties. Thankfully, they were able to stabilize her without the need for intubation, and she was admitted to the Pediatrics ICU.

During this time, my husband received news that his work travel date had to be moved up to that same evening. I knew then that the week ahead would be quite challenging. The next day, I had a scheduled meeting with my pastor, during which he prayed for grace for me. Although I didn't feel anything tangible at the moment, I later realized that a significant impartation had taken place.

Our daughter remained in the hospital from December 12th to January 1st. Despite the circumstances, my husband was still able to travel for work, and I managed to attend the School of Ministry graduation, fulfill work obligations, serve and fellowship at church, and enjoy holiday gatherings—all while making daily visits to the hospital, sometimes multiple times a day. This was truly remarkable, as I could have easily been tempted to cancel everything and become completely absorbed with my daughter's care while neglecting the others.

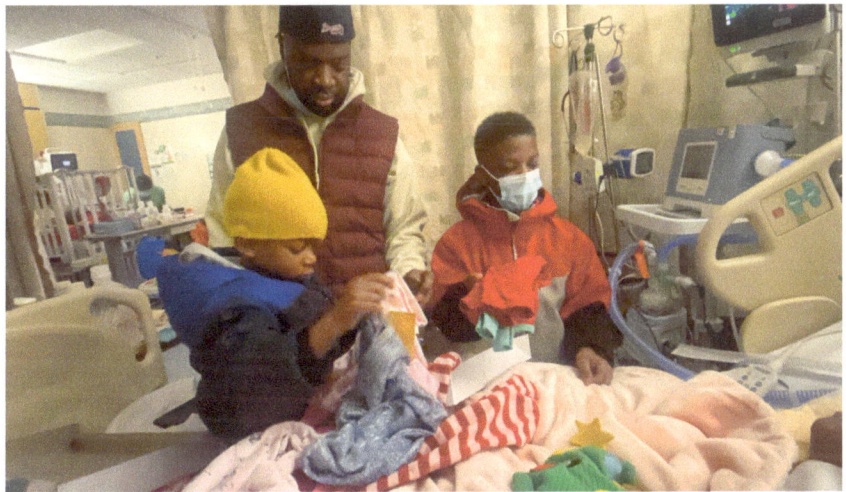

I recall leaving my eldest daughter in the hospital on Christmas Day after her delivery, but this time, God's grace enabled me to manage these unforeseen circumstances so effectively that the enemy attempted to make me feel guilty for keeping it together.

At one point, I encountered a nurse whose behaviour seemed questionable. Previously, I would have requested her removal, but I chose to remain calm. Miraculously, within five minutes, another nurse approached me and introduced herself, explaining that she was taking over because the previous nurse had been called to another case. It was a clear indication of God's intervention and provision.

Throughout this experience, God has been teaching me the importance of trusting Him to take care of His children, fighting our battles, and experiencing true rest and peace. Despite the challenges and tough lessons, I am thankful that God's grace never fails. Thank you, Jesus, for healing, peace, grace, and for always being faithful.

This marked Marie's third trip to the hospital under urgent circumstances. The second visit was prompted by mild flu-like symptoms, while the third unfolded with a bit more drama, leaving a lasting impression on me.

It all happened in June 2019. Marie began experiencing muscle spasms resembling a minor seizure, prompting a call from the daycare urging us to take her to the emergency room. Initially, we weren't overly concerned, as she occasionally displayed similar behaviour at home, seemingly signalling discomfort. However, daycare rules required a doctor's clearance for her return. Upon arriving at the emergency room, there was quite a commotion, with medical staff reacting as if she were seizing. Our initial relief turned to surprise as we realized the gravity of the situation. Hours later, it turned out she hadn't been seizing at all; rather, it was just muscle spasms, as we had suspected. Unfortunately, prior to this clarification, she had been given two seizure medications unnecessarily. This led to what was supposed to be a quick visit, turning into a longer stay to address the complications caused by the medications. One of the medications, which she didn't actually need, caused her body temperature to drop dangerously low, shifting the focus of the visit to restoring her temperature to normal levels.

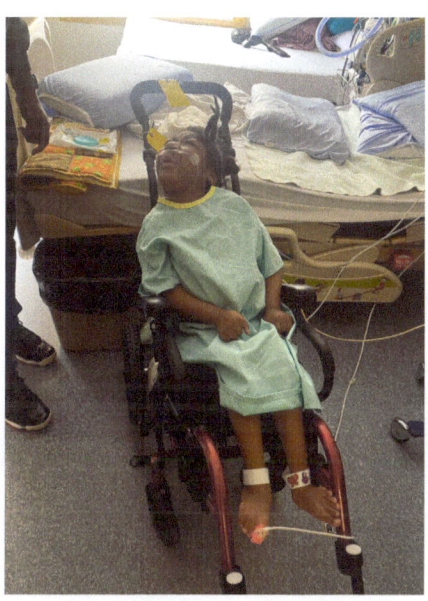

As a result, I was deeply affected by the experience. My trust in the hospital system plummeted, and I found myself reluctant to return for any reason. Fortunately, in the years that followed, our visits were limited to necessary tests or specialized appointments. Through it all, I couldn't help but feel grateful for God's protection over Marie. Despite her severe cerebral palsy diagnosis, she remained remarkably healthy. When we did return for the third time, many doctors expressed surprise at not having encountered her before. Some even commended us for maintaining her health, noting that individuals with multiple complications often require frequent medical attention. However, I couldn't attribute her well-being solely to our efforts. It was clear to me that it was God who had sustained her and guided us through it all.

However, this marked the beginning of an incredibly eventful seven months. Within that time frame, we found ourselves making four separate trips to the hospital during Marie's final months with us on Earth. Life was already bustling with activity, especially as my husband had just embarked on a new job. With much of the responsibility at home falling on my shoulders, adding these hospital visits felt like an overwhelming burden on top of everything else. How were we going to manage? It truly felt like a season of enduring hardship.

During this challenging period, Marie ended up spending both Christmas and her birthday in the hospital. It was a stark reminder of the unpredictability of life and the fragility of our circumstances.

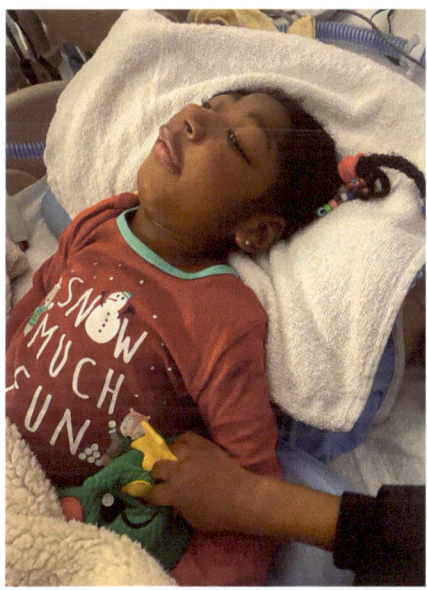

This season tested our love, patience, and resilience as parents. Despite being emotionally invested in Marie's health and recovery, we had to balance being her advocate amidst the complexity of her condition. We had to discern when to trust the doctors' plans and when to assert ourselves. Navigating through the obstacles of physical limitations, communication barriers, and societal misconceptions required both grace and determination. And even amidst all this, we had to ensure that our love and support for Marie and our other children remained unwavering. Through it all, we held onto our faith in God, knowing that He would see us through.

Indeed, situations that demand long-suffering truly illuminate our dependence on God in every aspect of life. This was undoubtedly one of those instances. Transitioning from a relatively low frequency of hospital visits to a sudden surge within a short span was undeniably exhausting. Yet, strangely, we found ourselves less stressed than in previous years when facing less complicated challenges.

Long suffering has a way of deepening our trust in God. It's in these moments of endurance that we're compelled to rely on His strength and guidance. Despite our fervent prayers, we often find ourselves confronted with circumstances that seem overwhelming. It's during these times that we utter prayers like, "God, I need your help to get through this; I need your grace, Jesus!"

Through it all, we learn to surrender our burdens to Him, knowing that He alone can provide the peace and strength we need to persevere.

"Dear brothers and sisters, when troubles of any kind come your way, consider it an opportunity for great joy. For you know that when your faith is tested, your endurance has a chance to grow. So let it grow, for when your endurance is fully developed, you will be perfect and complete, needing nothing."
James 1:2-4 NLT

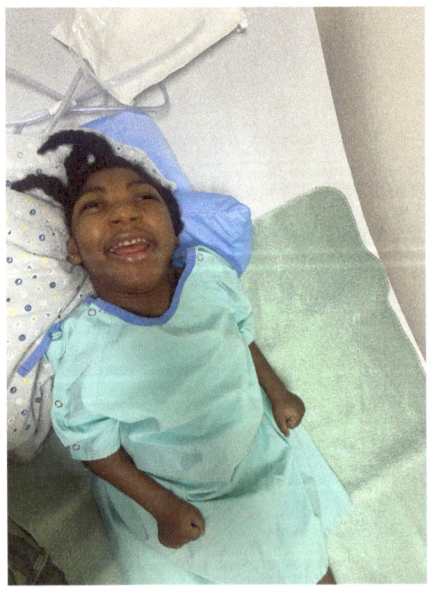

5

Transition to Glory

The echo of those dreaded words from the paramedics still reverberates within me: "I'm so sorry for your loss." Never did I imagine I would hear those words uttered about any of my children. It was utterly heart-wrenching—absolutely devastating. What happened to our plans, dear Jesus? We believed You would make her whole. She was meant to bring lives to You. We envisioned people seeing her transformation from before to after and rushing to embrace Your love. This was not the ending we envisioned. None of it made sense.

We were in the midst of a significant transition, searching for the perfect home tailored to Marie's needs. A home with a full bath and a bedroom on the main floor—a sanctuary for her. And miraculously, we found it. On the very day we were meant to move in, Marie left us.

The movers had just finished moving the last piece of furniture into the house. We had been carrying smaller items and boxes there periodically over the last few days, but this was the day all of the furniture would come. This was meant to be our first night sleeping in the new home.

Then we got a call to hurry and come now. Marie was unresponsive, and the paramedics were on their way. She was about 20 minutes away from us, where we were at the new house. We were blocked in the driveway by the movers' truck, and I remember shouting at them to move so we could leave immediately. I promised to pay them later but stressed the urgency of the situation. The 20-minute drive felt like an eternity, with every roadblock and traffic jam adding to the stress.

I reached out to a family friend closer to Marie's location while my husband drove. At the same time, I messaged our pastors and my mom, asking for their prayers and support. When we arrived, CPR had been ongoing for at least 15 minutes, with medical professionals working tirelessly. We knelt by Marie's side, holding her hand and praying with all our hearts.

I held onto hope for a miracle, believing that if Marie revived, she would be completely healed. However, after about 30 minutes of CPR, the paramedics delivered the heartbreaking news that reviving her heartbeat was unlikely. They suggested consulting a doctor over the phone to decide whether to continue efforts since taking her to the hospital seemed pointless. With heavy hearts, we agreed to their recommendation.

As more time passed, CPR efforts persisted. This part of the book was particularly challenging to write, by the way. Anyway, I vividly recall one paramedic working tirelessly to revive Marie, giving her all. The paramedic was a lady. Then, gradually, the voices around us fell silent until only one paramedic remained speaking, this same lady. I glanced around and realized they were trying to get her attention. I saw one of the paramedics say to her, "That's it..." and she responded with an "Oh..." For a moment, there was a deafening silence. I now understand firsthand the weight of deadly silence—a chilling quiet that filled the air. But it lasted only for a split second. It was then that Marie's spirit departed from her body.

A close elder who was present later described seeing a quick "swish" of Marie's spirit ascending up to heaven; almost as if she was in a rush.

Then came the painful condolences, one by one, and we all began to weep. It felt so surreal—how could something like this even happen? That morning would mark the last time I saw my precious girl awake.

She never did set foot inside the house. The home that was sought for so long, mainly with her in mind. It felt as though she had played a trick on us, knowing she would leave and wanting us to complete our home search list, even though she would never live there. She had bestowed the home upon us as a final gift before departing. If only we had known, we would have settled for less when moving in, and our search would have been less specific and extensive. So many things would have looked different if we had known. But we didn't.

I often find myself grappling with the question, "Why?". While some answers have been revealed to me, and while I try to focus on the positives, there are still many aspects that remain unclear. So many "whys?" linger in my mind. Yet, amidst the uncertainty, I choose to place my trust in the Creator who crafted both me and Marie. "I make known the end from the beginning, from ancient times, what is still to come," He declares. *"My purpose will stand, and I will do all that I please"* **Isaiah 46:10.**

If I can summon the faith to believe in a higher power beyond what I can physically see, then I must also embrace the belief that He knows what is ultimately best for me; and best for her. While we can attempt to decipher God's intentions and predict outcomes, who are we to comprehend the ways of God? *"'For my thoughts are not your thoughts, neither are your ways my ways,' declares the Lord* "**Isaiah 55:8.**

This journey is leading me to new depths of surrender, grace, trust, and rest.

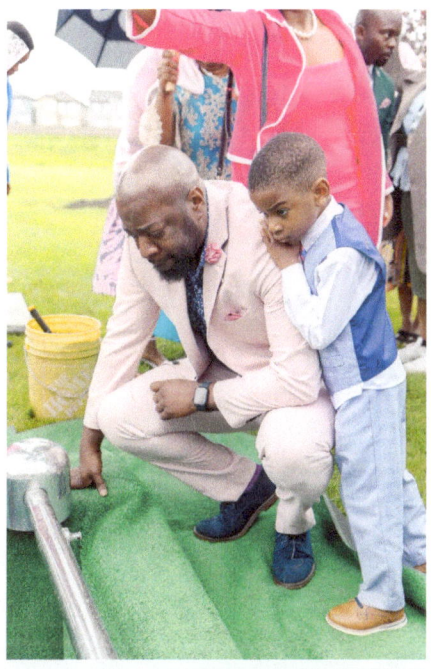

6

Surrender

Surrender is the act of giving up or handing over (a person, right, or possession), typically on compulsion or demand).

Surrendering weaves a thread of profound trust in the hands of the Divine.

To surrender to God's will is to realize that while we have control over our own actions, we actually don't have full control over the results of our actions. Surrendering to God's plan and allowing His process to play out embraces the idea and truth that there is a bigger and greater plan beyond our limited perspective. Surrender invites us to relinquish all resistance and flow along with God's plan.

Surrender is an act of humility, recognizing that our level of understanding is minute compared to the grand plan that our Heavenly Father has created for our lives. Doubt and worry are bound to creep into situations that may be difficult to comprehend, but through surrender, we place our faith in God's divine plan and trust that everything will unfold with perfect timing and purpose according to His will. Surrender is not a sign of weakness or giving up, but rather, it is a testament to our strength in relinquishing the need for ultimate control over our situation and the understanding that God truly knows best.

I've experienced surrendering a person, a right, and possession. Surrender is not necessarily fun. It could possibly mean giving up on a lifelong dream or desire. If you think about war, usually an army surrenders when they know they can't win. It's when they truly look around and realize that they are outnumbered. They can also choose not to fight. Some parents usually surrender their children to God after they realize they really can't help them. And then it's probably just the aspect of the "struggle" that is surrendered. At least, that's what I did a lot. We make certain decisions for our children without consulting God, and when our backs are against the wall, we say, "Lord, this is your child; do what only you can do. Once things seem under control again, we may start making decisions that He should be making again. We need to get to a place of full surrender in all areas of our lives, including parenting.

It is in letting go that we discover a profound sense of peace, knowing that we are held by God's love and that love will never allow our destinies to be destroyed. In the loving embrace of a universal force that guides us with unwavering grace. Through surrender, we transcend the limitations of our human minds and align ourselves with the infinite intelligence that shapes our destinies.

As we surrender to God's will, we surrender to the highest good that transcends our individual desires and fears. It is a sacred surrender that invites us to step into the flow of divine grace, where every twist and turn of life's journey becomes a sacred dance of surrender and trust. In this surrender, we find the freedom to be fully present in each moment, knowing that we are guided by a wisdom far greater than our own.

May we embrace the path of surrender with open hearts and minds, trusting in the divine plan that unfolds with beauty and grace. In surrendering to God's will, we discover the true essence of faith and love and the profound interconnectedness that unites us all in the tapestry of creation.

7

Grace

Testimony - August 2023

I'm here to thank God for His grace.

April this year was our month of abundant grace. My Senior Pastor said during one service that nothing that would happen that week could keep us down. This was also my birthday month, and I told God I needed a super level of this grace. I also held onto this word beyond that week.

The following month of May was filled with hospital stays and various illnesses among my family members. It felt so hard, but I was so grateful to make it to the month of June alive and with my mental health intact. I asked God for a drama-free June, and of course, it wasn't. It involved a flood in the basement and many more unexpected happenings. Yet God's grace still prevailed, and we made it to July.

That month, I said I would not ask for drama-free but for the grace to deal with whatever comes. I realize that I truly didn't know what I was asking for, but He delivered. July came with gut-punching, heart-wrenching drama and trauma that no parent ever wants to have to deal with. On July 13th, one month later, our youngest daughter passed away and transitioned to glory. She was buried on July 26th, 2024. So many emotions, unexpected tasks, expenses, and questions arose from this event. Yet, we have made it to August. There are many aspects of this testimony that I'm sure I will share here in the future and on many other platforms. But today is a testimony of God's grace. I pondered if it was too early to share this testimony, but what we give thanks for multiplies, and I know I will need much more grace to face the new reality.

God's grace is real and tangible. It is especially available here in this movement (Cornerstone Christian Church of God). I would not be standing up here talking without it. Beyond tapping into my grace channel, I've learned to consciously pull grace and strength from my spiritual parents, my family, and my friends.

Our family has experienced many heavy challenges over the years, some simultaneously, yet God has and still is keeping us. No matter your situation, anxiety and depression are real; isolation is not the answer! Tap into the grace that is available here, tap into the word, the community, begin serving in a ministry, and join a life group; you have a support system here. This is part one of many but I will leave you with the words of Paul.

"But by the grace of God I am what I am, and His grace toward me was not in vain, but I laboured more abundantly than they all, yet not I, but the grace of God which was with me." **1 Corinthians 15:10 NKJV**

There is grace available in God.

"And He said to me, 'My grace is sufficient for you, for My strength is made perfect in weakness.' Therefore most gladly I will rather boast in my infirmities, that the power of Christ may rest upon me. Therefore I take pleasure in infirmities, in reproaches, in needs, in persecutions, in distresses, for Christ's sake. For when I am weak, then I am strong." **2 Corinthians 12:9-10. NKJV**

In this passage, our brother Paul speaks about the thorn in his flesh that he was given. Even without fully understanding what was happening, one thing is clear: it was an ongoing uncomfortable situation for some reason. Yet, he accepted God's response that His grace was enough for him. God expressed that His strength is made perfect in weakness.

Despite what worldly thought might suggest, it is possible to move on after losing a loved one. Notice I said loved one; the fact that there is the capability to keep moving forward after a loved one's passing does not discount the love you have for them.

Losing someone close to you can indeed bring about feelings of "weakness". It can drain your energy, create a hollow feeling in your stomach, and leave you feeling very tired and weak. This is precisely the time to rely on the strength from above.

The pain I experienced when Marie transitioned was arguably enough to make me want to curl up in bed and forget the rest of the world. Yet, God provided grace to keep moving forward and for a speedy healing. Looking back, I sometimes wonder, "How in the world did I get through that time?" I had so many mixed emotions, so many questions, so much pain, yet God's grace saw me through. It feels almost unreal.

This same grace has carried my family through challenge after challenge, doctor visit after doctor visit. It propelled me through days when I barely had any sleep and was running on fumes.

8

Rest

Testimony - Dec 2021

I would like to thank God for restoring my vision. Over the past 4 years, I experienced severe burnout. Due to the mishandling of my youngest daughter's testimony in the works, the sleep deprivation and emotional roller coasters that some women experience after delivery for a few weeks to a few months, I endured for over 4 years. Unwisely, I took this on personally, physically, emotionally, and mentally. I felt it was my duty to fix everything. But I didn't recognize that I was idolizing her and the situation, taking on what I literally could not fix and trying to do God's job. This severe burnout affected everyone and everything close to me.

2 years ago, it was "highly advised," aka instructed, that we take her to our "home" country, The Bahamas, for a period of time in order to regroup. To me, this was absolutely not an option. In fact, it was absurd. As far as I knew, this was my child, and it was my duty to care for her. So, I continued doing the same thing, expecting a different result. Last year, 2 days after returning from a retreat, I felt so exhausted, like I never went, and I debriefed with Pastor Ibukun about it. I thought I just needed help with structure, but she could see what I couldn't see and escalated the situation to Pastor Emmanuel, who

brought up the instruction once again. In his words, I was walking through the valley of the shadow of death, and my body was defining the laws of nature. But this time, the Grace was running out.

Long story short, this time, I obliged. Even though it was temporary, it would be hard, but life was already hard anyway. It's been about 4 months now, and during that short time, God has accelerated revelation, clarified spiritual identity, restored the vision He gave, and birthed the movement Women's Intermission, a mission set to encourage women to do what I had failed to do for years; Love and take care of themselves before they can do the same for others. He reminded me that I'm just a caretaker of His children and that He knows best for me and them.

God knew what he wanted me to do and went to the extreme of temporarily separating me from a child I carried for 9 months to ensure first that I didn't lose my mind and second that His will was done. I challenge you to focus on what God has asked you to do, not on the challenges. Someone's destiny is dependent on your obedience.

Life's most challenging situations can often leave us feeling overwhelmed, stressed, and utterly drained. In the midst of such trials, finding rest in Christ may seem like an elusive dream. Yet, it is precisely in these moments of intense difficulty that the rest found in Christ becomes most vital. It's a refuge from the storms, a sanctuary for the weary soul. But what does it truly mean to rest in Christ?

Resting in Christ is more than just finding physical relaxation; it's a profound spiritual posture, a surrendering of our anxieties and burdens to the One who holds all things together. It's an acknowledgment that despite the turmoil around us, we can find peace in His presence.

Life's challenges don't magically disappear when we choose to rest in Christ. Trials still come, and storms still rage. Resting in Christ during challenging times involves surrendering our burdens to Him. It's acknowledging that we cannot carry the weight of our troubles alone and entrusting them into His capable hands. It allows us to tap into God's strength, which is infinitely greater than our own.

"And he said unto me, My grace is sufficient for thee: for my strength is made perfect in weakness. Most gladly therefore will I rather glory in my infirmities, that the power of Christ may rest upon me." **2 Corinthians 12:9 NLT**

Finding rest in Christ means anchoring ourselves in His promises. It's holding onto the assurance that God is with us in the storm, that He will never leave us nor forsake us. Resting in Christ involves seeking His presence through prayer and meditation. In the midst of life's storms, spending time in communion with God brings a sense of peace that transcends understanding. It's in these moments of quiet reflection that we are reminded of God's faithfulness, His goodness, and His unwavering love for us.

It is extremely important to seek a word to hold on to regarding your situation. This word allows for hope and stability in the midst of chaos.

Additionally, resting in Christ requires self-care. It's important to prioritize our physical, emotional, and mental well-being, even in the midst of adversity. This may involve setting boundaries, seeking support from loved ones, and practicing healthy coping mechanisms to manage stress. It may also involve getting adequate physical rest, eating balanced meals, exercising, and getting massages.

While challenging situations may test our faith and endurance, they also provide an opportunity to experience the rest that can only be found in Christ. By surrendering our burdens, anchoring ourselves in His promises, seeking His presence, prioritizing self-care, and trusting in His sovereignty, we can navigate life's storms with grace and peace.

Resting in Christ is a journey - a journey of learning to trust, of letting go, and of finding peace in the midst of life's uncertainties. It's a journey worth embarking on - a journey that leads us ever closer to the heart of our Savior. It is not a passive act; it's an intentional choice we make every day. It's a continual surrendering of our will to His, a constant turning to Him for strength and guidance.

9

Trust

Faith and trust are distinct yet interconnected aspects of our relationship with God. As believers in Christ, we inherently possess a level of faith, as it takes faith to believe in God's existence even though we cannot see Him. However, trust is something that is cultivated over time through our experiences and observations of God's faithfulness in our lives.

Building trust in God can be expedited when we reflect on His track record of keeping His promises and delivering us from past challenges. While faith can be developed through prayer, seeking the guidance of the Holy Spirit, and immersing ourselves in His Word, trust grows as we witness His faithfulness in action.

It's essential to recognize that building faith solely in the things God promises to do for us is only part of the journey. True growth occurs when we cultivate faith in God simply because He is God—when we trust in His sovereignty and goodness, regardless of whether or not His actions align with our expectations or desires.

Listening to and meditating on the Word of God are crucial aspects of strengthening our faith, as Romans 10:17 reminds us that faith comes from hearing the Good News about Christ.

Ultimately, building faith in God involves moving beyond believing in His promises to trusting in His character and sovereignty, even when our prayers are not answered in the way we hoped. It's about having unwavering trust that God always has our best interests at heart, even in the face of disappointment or unanswered prayers. This level of trust—faith in God simply because He is God—is the pinnacle of our spiritual growth.

Absolutely, Romans 8:28 reminds us that God orchestrates all things for the good of those who love Him and are called according to His purpose. This underscores the importance of aligning ourselves with God's will and seeking His guidance to discern which parts of His Word are applicable to each season of our lives.

While God's Word is unchanging and trustworthy, there are indeed times and seasons when different aspects of His Word resonate with us more deeply or are particularly relevant to our circumstances. Therefore, receiving direction and revelation from God regarding His will for our lives is crucial in ensuring that we are always in alignment with His plan.

By seeking God's guidance and allowing Him to reveal His purposes to us, we can navigate through life's various seasons with confidence and assurance, knowing that His Word will guide us and His will for our lives will ultimately lead to our good and His glory.

As Jeremiah 1:5 affirms, God knew us even before we were formed in our mother's womb, setting us apart for His specific purpose. This intimate knowledge and divine foresight surpass any human understanding or relationship. Indeed, while we place varying degrees of trust in our spouses, doctors, coaches, pastors, and friends, it should be minor in comparison to the trust we have in God. They all have their limitations and imperfections, but God's knowledge and understanding exceed human comprehension.

When reflecting on our relationships, many people often recall their first memories of meeting someone, such as "when we first met" or "the first time I saw you." However, there's someone who can say, "I knew you before I even formed you!" The fact that God knew us even before we were conceived, before our existence, underscores the intimate and eternal nature of His relationship with us. He knows every aspect of our being, including our thoughts, feelings, and desires.

This profound knowledge and understanding demonstrate the depth of God's love for us and His unwavering commitment to our well-being. He alone can guide us through life's challenges and uncertainties with grace and assurance, for He is the one who formed us and knows us intimately.

Just as meticulous planning and investment are involved in constructing a building with a specific purpose, God serves as the visionary, architect, and investor of our lives. He has intricately designed us to fulfill His purpose, knowing exactly how we need to be built and even sacrificing His Son's life for our salvation.

Therefore, we can confidently place our trust in God. He has a clear vision for our lives and is intimately involved in every aspect of our existence. His faithfulness, wisdom, and love far exceed any human capacity for trust. He has invested His blameless Son's death for our lives, making Him wholly worthy of our trust.

Take a pledge today to place your trust in Jesus, regardless of how dire the situation may appear. The Bible teaches us that the earth is merely the Lord's footstool, indicating the vastness of His power and perspective. Even with perfect vision, our sight cannot rival His. He holds the ultimate wisdom and insight into your future. Therefore, rest assured, He is trustworthy.

10

Gratitude

Testimony - Jan 2024

I want to begin by expressing my heartfelt gratitude to God for once again preserving my life. Around 7 years ago, I faced a terrifying ordeal with placental abruption and internal bleeding towards the end of my pregnancy. The doctor's words echoed in my mind: "Your body was literally trying to kill itself." I never take for granted the fact that God intervened and spared my life during that critical time.

Reflecting on the past year, I must admit it felt heavy and overwhelming at times. It seemed like 2023 presented my family with a myriad of health challenges, rejections, and moments of grief, among other trials. However, in the midst of it all, I received valuable advice from my pastor on how to find gratitude in every situation. He taught me that if I know how to think, I also know how to "thank".

From this perspective, I want to take a moment to thank God for the year 2023. Despite its difficulties, it has been a year of remarkable growth, elevation, and revelation for me. I have experienced emotional and physical healing, and God has taken me on a journey to deepen my trust in Him, even when I don't understand His ways. Moreover, He has shown me the importance of bringing my troubles to Him first before anyone else.

This year has also been marked by profound losses, as both my daughter and my longest friend gained their heavenly crowns. Yet, amidst these tragic situations, God has used them to reveal more about my calling and to strengthen my resolve for the path He has set before me. Through it all, I have learned to lean on His grace and to find hope in His promises.

Reflecting on Marie's final years with us has been definitely challenging. However, as I've managed to navigate through the emotions and truly examine all that unfolded, I can sincerely declare, "To God be the Glory, Great Things He has done!"

No, I'm not delusional. Despite the difficulties and the prolonged period of enduring hardship, so many aspects could have spiraled out of control. Through it all, I've come to understand the power of gratitude. Even in the midst of suffering, finding something to be thankful for, even if it requires a meticulous search, is crucial for maintaining resilience and lifting one's spirits.

I deliberately included various testimonies that I had shared at my church over the years in this book because it can be challenging to recognize God's goodness during times of extreme difficulty. However, our Heavenly Father is constantly at work! He is always doing something worthy of our gratitude.

Gratitude acts as a beacon of light amidst the darkness, reminding us of the blessings and the silver linings amidst the trials. It's a practice that shifts our focus from despair to hope, from sorrow to joy. So, yes, amidst the pain and the struggles, I choose to be grateful, for it is through gratitude that I find strength and resilience to persevere.

"Even though the fig trees have no blossoms, and there are no grapes on

the vines; even though the olive crop fails, and the fields lie empty and barren; even though the flocks die in the fields, and the cattle barns are empty, yet I will rejoice in the Lord! I will be joyful in the God of my salvation!"
Habakkuk 3:17-18 NLT

Acknowledging even the smallest blessings can provide moments of relief, comfort, and strength amidst adversity. It's a testament to God's goodness, which remains steadfast regardless of our circumstances. He is always good, without exception.

God indeed encourages us to cultivate an attitude of gratitude in every situation. It's a powerful practice that shifts our perspective from focusing solely on our challenges to recognizing the abundance of blessings that surround us, even in difficult times.

By choosing gratitude, we align ourselves with God's will and open ourselves to His peace and provision, even amidst life's storms. It's a reminder that no matter what we face, God's goodness and faithfulness endure, offering us hope and encouragement along the journey.

"Always be joyful. Never stop praying. Be thankful in all circumstances, for this is God's will for you who belong to Christ Jesus."
1 Thessalonians 5:16-18 NLT

During tough times, it's crucial to keep these important benefits of gratitude in mind. They'll help you stay afloat amidst challenges and prevent becoming overwhelmed. Gratitude can be a powerful tool for navigating through challenges in several ways:

Shifts Perspective
Expressing gratitude helps us shift our focus from what's going wrong to what's going right. It allows us to see the positives amidst

the negatives and helps us recognize the blessings, no matter how small they may seem.

Promotes Resilience

When we practice gratitude, we acknowledge the good things in our lives, which can boost our resilience in the face of adversity. It reminds us of our past victories and strengths, giving us the confidence to tackle present challenges.

Fosters Positive Emotions

Gratitude cultivates positive emotions such as joy, hope, and contentment. These emotions can counteract feelings of fear, anxiety, and despair that often accompany challenging situations, helping us maintain a more balanced emotional state.

Strengthens Relationships

Expressing gratitude fosters a sense of connection and appreciation in our relationships. During tough times, the support of loved ones can provide comfort and encouragement, reinforcing your resilience.

Encourages Problem-Solving

When we approach challenges with a grateful mindset, we become more open to seeking solutions and finding opportunities for growth. Gratitude encourages a proactive approach to problem-solving rather than dwelling on setbacks.

Enhances Well-Being

Gratitude is linked to improved mental and physical well-being. It boosts mood, enhances sleep quality, and reduces symptoms of anxiety and depression, helping you maintain overall health and vitality.

In essence, gratitude serves as a guiding light during challenging times, helping us find hope, strength, and meaning even in the darkest moments of our lives.

11

Death

God entrusts us with the care of our children for a limited time before calling them back home. While physical death is a part of this process, there's also a spiritual aspect known as "death to self" that's crucial in our Christian journey. "Death to self" involves surrendering our own desires, ambitions, and will to God, putting aside selfishness and sinful tendencies to live according to Christ's teachings.

In **Galatians 2:20**, the apostle Paul emphasizes the transformative nature of faith in Christ. He encourages believers to embrace a spiritual rebirth by crucifying their old selves, symbolizing a profound change from a life driven by selfish desires and worldly ambitions to one characterized by faith and obedience to God. This process of crucifixion signifies a decisive break with the sinful patterns of the past, allowing for the emergence of a new life guided by the principles of the Gospel.

As parents, applying the concept of "death to self" takes on a profound significance in shaping our relationship with our children. It involves relinquishing our personal dreams and aspirations for our children and surrendering them to God's divine will. Rather than imposing our own agendas on their lives, we are called to trust in God's plan and purpose for each of our children. This requires humility, trust, and a willingness to let go of our own desires, allowing God to work in their lives according to His perfect wisdom and timing.

By embracing "death to self" as parents, we cultivate an attitude of surrender and submission to God's authority, recognizing that His plans far surpass our own. It enables us to parent from a place of faith and reliance on God's guidance, rather than from a position of control or manipulation. Ultimately, it fosters an environment where our children can freely pursue their God-given purpose and destiny, knowing that they are supported by our love and prayers, grounded in God's unfailing grace and wisdom.

Recently, I had a conversation with someone who candidly shared her experience of having big dreams for her son's future, only to realize that it may not align with his own aspirations. It's natural for parents to want success for their children, but our idea of success is often influenced by our own experiences and perspectives. Many parents base their definition of success on what they've witnessed in their lifetime or heard from previous generations, without seeking God's guidance for His plans for their children.

Death to self involves letting go of personal desires and attachments in order to grow closer to God, achieving a higher level of spiritual enlightenment. If we are so attached to our desires about a matter, and not willing to let go of them, it will be very difficult to accept anything that God is saying about that same matter, no matter how many times we say that we are seeking God's face about that matter.

So, **Luke 9:23** and **Galatians 5:24** are like the tag team champs when it comes to explaining "death to self".

In **Luke 9:23**, Jesus delivers a straightforward message, emphasizing the necessity of self-denial for those who choose to follow Him. Taking up one's cross daily symbolizes a commitment to prioritize Jesus' teachings and directives over personal desires and comforts. It's a call to embrace the challenges and sacrifices that come with discipleship, recognizing that true fulfillment lies wholeheartedly following Christ's path. It's like picking up your cross every single day and saying, "Yep, I'm all in, Jesus!" It means ditching your own plans and comfort zones to follow the path He's carved out for you. It's not always easy, but it's the real deal when it comes to living out your faith.

Then there's **Galatians 5:24**, a reality check: If you're on Team Jesus, there is no option but to put your old selfish desires and passions six feet under. It's like saying goodbye to your old ways and embracing a whole new life where Jesus is calling the shots. It's a total transformation from the inside out, thanks to what Jesus did for us on the cross. This spiritual death to our selfish inclinations opens the door to a life characterized by righteousness, obedience, and spiritual growth.

So, when you're feeling torn between your own desires and what God's got in store for you, remember these verses. They're like your playbook for living a life that's all about Jesus - a life of practicing self-denial and crucifying our fleshly desires daily to cultivate a deeper intimacy with Christ.

Jesus had to endure the agony of the cross so that we could have a shot at a better life. His sacrifice was huge—dying for our sins, bringing us peace, and healing our brokenness. It wasn't easy, but Jesus had to make that sacrifice so that the Holy Spirit could come and be with us. It's like His sacrifice opened up a whole new level of connection between us and God.

When we think about Jesus giving up everything for us, it puts our own desires into perspective. Sometimes, what we want might seem right to us, but Jesus' sacrifice shows us that God's plan is always better - even if it doesn't make sense to us at the time. So, when we're struggling with our own wants and needs, we can look to Jesus' sacrifice as a reminder that God's plan is the best plan, even when it's hard to see.

Realizing some key truths has certainly eased the burdens of this journey. First and foremost, we understand that children ultimately belong to Jesus and that we're merely caretakers entrusted with their well-being. Recognizing that His ways and plans surpass our understanding and that He sees the end from the beginning brings a sense of peace and trust.

In any partnership, each participant has their own role to fulfill. It's like in a dance where each person has their steps to follow. However, we often find ourselves trying to take on tasks that aren't ours to bear, especially in our partnership with God. We end up trying to do His job instead of focusing on our own responsibilities.

Our role is to speak and declare The Word, what we desire to see and then trust God to handle the rest. We're meant to engage with faith, activating the power of ministering angels through our words. When we worry and try to micromanage the situation, we essentially tie God's hands, hindering His ability to work freely.

It's only when we release our grip and allow God to take charge that we'll see the fruits of our faith. So, let's speak boldly, trust wholeheartedly, and watch as God orchestrates His perfect plan in our lives and in the lives of our children.

12

Merely Caretakers

Testimony - Jan 2024

I'm here to express my heartfelt gratitude for the realignment of my identity. It's important for me to share some details of this testimony in the hope that it may help others on their own journeys. You see, my previous middle name had a rather negative connotation—it meant "one that draws water, poverty, cloud, death." Interestingly, it also happened to be the name of one of Haman's sons in the Bible, who met a tragic end due to his father's actions. Unfortunately, my life seemed to reflect some negative aspects associated with that name.

When my mother chose this name for me, she did so with good intentions. At the time, she was a born-again Christian and selected it from a concordance because it resembled her own middle name. She spoke countless declarations over my life throughout the years. However, despite no one ever calling me by my middle name, its symbolism still haunted me.

I share this to highlight the importance of being informed about the significance of names. Sometimes, even with the best intentions, we can inadvertently miss important details. I am deeply grateful for my mother's humility and *spiritual maturity. She gave her blessing for me to change my name, apologized to me, and repented before God. I understand that not everyone experiences such understanding and support.*

Recently, my 5-year-old son expressed a desire to change his name, citing that everyone else seemed to be doing it. While we laughed it off, it sparked a conversation about the significance of names being given by God. I'll admit it made me uneasy at first. What if my children one day decide to change their names? However, in that moment, God reassured me and brought me peace about their identities and destinies. I later recommitted a difficult vow to God that whatever it takes for my children to fulfill their destiny, I will do my best to conform.

As a child, I urge others to seek God's guidance about their names if they haven't already. Changing names isn't merely a trend; it's about embracing one's true identity and fulfilling destiny. Destinies are attached to your true identity.

To fellow parents, especially those with adult children, I encourage you to release your children and their destinies into God's hands. We may strive for perfection as parents, but we are not infallible. If mistakes have been made, accept them, repent, and allow God to redeem and rescue their destinies.

Though it's challenging to navigate as an adult, it's never too late to seek enlightenment and realignment. I am immensely grateful to the Lord for replacing my middle name with one that represents grace and favour.

Caretakers: I stumbled upon various definitions of the term "caretaker," ranging from providing physical or emotional care and support to being employed to look after people or animals. However, one particular definition caught my attention:

"Holding power temporarily..."

The emphasis on "temporarily" in this definition was intriguing. It made me reflect on the cultural and societal norms I grew up with, where parents often made statements like:

"I brought you into this world and can take you out."
"Until you are of age, you belong to me."
"This child is my one good seed... my everything."

While these phrases might seem common or even authoritative, they carry inherent dangers. Sometimes, we say things without fully understanding their implications, or we echo what we've heard from others.

First and foremost, while parents play a vital role in the creation of their children, there is a higher power at play. A Master who determines the outcome, deciding whether all our efforts were in vain or not. This Master dictates precisely how many attempts it takes for the egg implantation process to succeed.

> "Behold, children are a heritage from the Lord, The fruit of the womb is a reward." **Psalm 127:3 NKJV**

> "Children are a gift from the Lord; they are a reward from him."
> **Psalms 127:3 NLT**

Heritage and gift are two powerful concepts intertwined when it comes to children and parenting. Heritage speaks of the special possessions and legacies passed down from generation to generation. It's about the traditions, values, and connections that shape a family's identity. When it comes to children, they inherit not just genes but also the hopes and dreams of God.

On the other hand, a gift is something given willingly, without expecting anything in return. Children are precious gifts from God, blessings bestowed upon parents with love and intention. They bring joy, meaning, and purpose to their families' lives.

In essence, children belong first and foremost to God. While parents play a role in their upbringing, the decision to bless them with children ultimately rests with the divine. Whether through natural conception or adoption, each child is a unique expression of God's grace and providence.

Ceremonies like Christening or Baby Dedication take on special significance. They're not just about tradition but about acknowledging the divine origin of children and committing to raise them in accordance with God's will. It's a solemn declaration of stewardship, recognizing the sacred responsibility of nurturing and guiding these precious gifts from above.

When we submit in this way, we are embracing and surrendering to God's unique plan for each child's life. It's about acknowledging that God's plan transcends our own ambitions and desires for our children. Instead of imposing our dreams of them taking over the family business, becoming the first doctor in the family, or attending prestigious universities, we are called to align with God's purpose for their lives.

Of course, we want the best for our children. We're not passive spectators, simply saying, "Well, they're God's children, so I have no say." On the contrary, it's our responsibility as caretakers to take this role seriously. We've been entrusted by God to guide them toward their destinies.

Yet, it's crucial to seek God's vision for their lives. We should desire their success and elevation, but in the area that God has specifically called them to dominate. It's not about fulfilling our own aspirations through them, but about helping them discover and fulfill God's purpose for them.

Consider this: What if your daughter excels as the top point guard in the WNBA, but God intended her to be the world's top 100-meter sprinter? The difference may seem subtle, but in God's plan, every detail matters. It's about being in the right place at the right time, impacting lives according to God's ordained purpose.

In essence, understanding and aligning with God's plan for our children ensures that they fulfill their true purpose, impacting the world in ways far beyond what we could imagine. It's about recognizing that their purpose is intricately connected to God's timing and divine appointments.

It's natural for parents to feel deeply attached to their children. After all, a mother carries her baby for nine months, and we're encouraged to bond with them from the moment they're born. Yet, finding the balance between recognizing them as "our own" and understanding that they ultimately belong to God can be tricky.

Think of it like being a fun aunt or uncle tasked with temporary responsibility. You're in charge until the parents return, doing your best, but ultimately, the one who created them holds the greatest responsibility. So, when my kids are misbehaving, and I report them to their dad, I jokingly say, "Can you go and deal with your children?" It's a playful reminder that while they are our children, their mischievous antics might be traced back to him.

When it comes to meeting their needs, whether it's school fees, winter clothes, or anything else requiring financial support, I'm quick to turn to God and say, "Sir, these are your children. I dedicated them back to you, and you promised to provide for them." And without fail, He always comes through.

But it would be unfair and disrespectful of me to only turn to

God for financial needs. What about questions regarding their destiny? Discipline? Nutrition? Education? Navigating the teenage years? After all, their Heavenly Father created each of them with unique features and purposes.

My mom used to use this analogy when discussing destiny with me: If you're driving a car made by one company, would you consult the manual of another? Similarly, we sometimes act as if we know better than God, forgetting that He created us and knows what's best for us—let alone His children.

"'For I know the plans I have for you,' says the LORD. 'They are plans for good and not for disaster, to give you a future and a hope'". **Jeremiah 29:11 NLT**. This verse also applies to our children.

Learning to separate from my children in a healthy way has been quite the journey for me. It hit me hard when I realized that no matter how much I teach them about safety—stranger danger, crossing the street—there's just no way I can keep them completely safe. Unlike God, I can't be everywhere and see everything they do. Their Heavenly Father sees all, I don't. Those moments when I seem to magically know exactly what they're up to, that's God providing discernment.

I've come to trust my instincts. If I have reservations about a particular place or person and can't bring myself to separate from my kids for even a few hours, then I know it's not a safe environment. And that sense of peace? That's God's hand at work too. When I drop them off somewhere and feel that peace settles in, it's like a signal that it's okay to let go a bit. I'll never stop caring for them, never mistreat them, but part of raising healthy adults is trusting that God will guide them and help them make the right choices.

This understanding has been a lifeline for me in the grieving and healing processes. I have no doubt that my baby girl is with God, her Heavenly Father right now. If I can trust earthly caretakers with my children, how much more can I trust God? He knows her better than I ever could. So on those tough days, when the pain feels unbearable, I remind myself of this truth: I can never care for Marie better than her Heavenly Father can.

Matthew 6:8 NKJV says it best: *"...For your Father knows the things you have need of before you ask Him."* If God knows exactly what we need here on earth, how much more does He know the needs of one of His newest angels? When the ache sets in, I find solace in knowing that Marie is in the best hands possible.

13

Higher Ways

Remember when I had it all planned out? Well, at least I thought I did. Marie was supposed to be healed right here on earth; her healing to be a miracle that would leave the skeptics stunned and countless souls would come to Christ. Her story would echo across the globe, touching hearts and transforming lives. But things didn't unfold that way, not even close. In fact, it often felt like the very things the skeptics predicted were coming to pass.

Yet, Marie was here with a mission, a purpose that transcended earthly understanding. And to be completely honest, I'm still piecing together the full extent of her purpose. Despite her silence, she spoke volumes. She knew what she wanted and had a unique way of making it known. Though she never took a step, she journeyed far and wide, leaving an indelible mark on countless lives. She led without force, shaping our family's decisions and guiding us with her unwavering will. She challenged us to strengthen our faith and forced us to grow in ways we never imagined. And though I may not grasp every detail of her purpose, I can confidently say she fulfilled it.

Consider this: God sent me here with a purpose, and He sent Marie with hers. Though I was her earthly caretaker, we are distinct individuals with unique assignments. One of Marie's purposes was to assist me in fulfilling my own calling. It would be a disservice to ignore the profound lessons she taught me, lessons that perhaps others could glean from her life. Could God truly send someone to earth for just six short years to impact others? What about their own life, their destiny? Yet, Jesus Himself walked the earth for only 33 years, fulfilling His purpose completely.

So why share all of this? Because when I view Marie not just as my daughter but as a fellow sister in Christ, a divine instrument in God's hands, some things begin to make sense. Though I may not grasp the entirety of God's plan, I can see how Marie's life has shaped me, teaching me empathy, resilience, and a deeper understanding of purpose. And just when I thought I couldn't find the next step in my journey, Marie's passing brought clarity and revelation. Did God have to take her from us so soon for me to grasp this truth? Perhaps not, but as my spiritual father often says, "There are many ways to get to Calgary from Edmonton." God's ways are beyond my comprehension, yet I trust that I will understand more in due time. Until then, I'll continue learning from my precious destiny helper.

14

Year 2023

That Year
I thought It came to break me
Came to shake me
Yet it built me up
It did break
It did shake
That year
Boundaries, bondages, capacity levels

Flesh, desires, selfish endevours
I wanted what I wanted
How I wanted
When
He said you are mine
So I say when
You think you are not ready
Yet it's time
You think you need more time
But now is the time
You are ready
You have what you need
You think there is more that you need
But I'm all that you need
I've always been there and I'll never leave
But she must leave...
And now
you must find you
And you must find me
Together a dynasty
We've conquered before
Yet there is much more
So we will do it again
And again
And again
That's what we do
We move
And never stop moving
That year
My time to learn what it means to have backing
The one I poured into most
Taken
My world shaken
What will I do with all of of this to give

Why did I outlive
Make it make sense
But it doesn't make sense
Will it ever make sense
Yet not nonsense
Strategic
Intentional
Yet Unconventional
Mandatory
Necessary
Statutory
Yet
Moments I thought would make me lose my mind
Made me find
That I'm stronger than I thought
Built different
Resilient
Made for war
Created to soar
High above the challenge
Because He that created me
Is bigger than the challenge
And He that's within me
Is greater
Than that of the world
That year
To him was no surprise
The all wise
Heard my cries
Dried my tears
Calmed my fears
Answered prayers
In His own way
For His own Glory

Truth
Re-playing back the moment
The moments
Over and over
And over and over
Again
Did this really actually happen?
Like did it really happen?
A piece of me gone
One that once lived inside of me
Taken
By the one that lives inside of me
Is that not selfish
Is that not cruel?
To teach me to love
To teach me to hope
Where there is life there is hope
Now no more hope
Yet there is still life
Eternal life
The life we've been promised
The life we labour to achieve
Achieved
Oh she laboured
From moment one
Fighting against time
Before they called it done
But she fought
And won
And then the true fight begun
Her fight
My fight
Her fight to stay alive
My fight to keep faith alive

Her fight to thrive
My fight to survive
The doctors reports
The prognosis
Many facts
One truth
In tug o' war
Team Facts were plenty
Team Truth was mighty
Bets on the truth
To prevail and win
To conquer the facts
To win the game
The game of life
It was over
But who did win?
Was this what facts predicted?
Did truth forfeit it?
I don't think I get it
Why did the match even exist?
The why daily unravelling
Snippets
Of this mystery
Of life given
Then taken
By the one licensed to give
And licensed to take
One day
The pieces will morph into a picture
That will tell a story
The ashes will rise in the wind
And create
Something beautiful
Truth has won

Memories

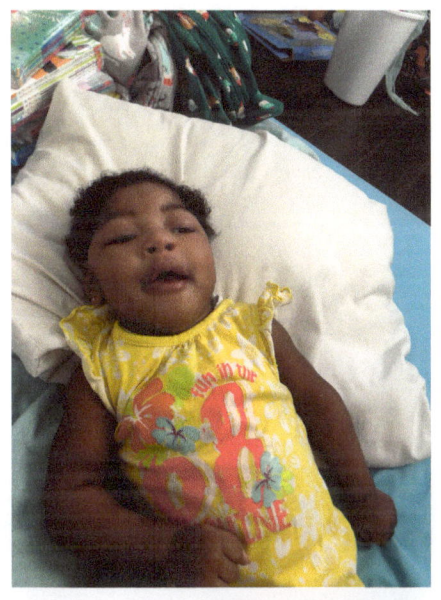

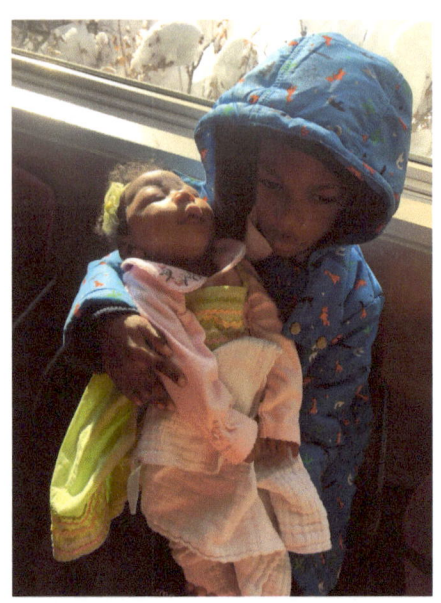
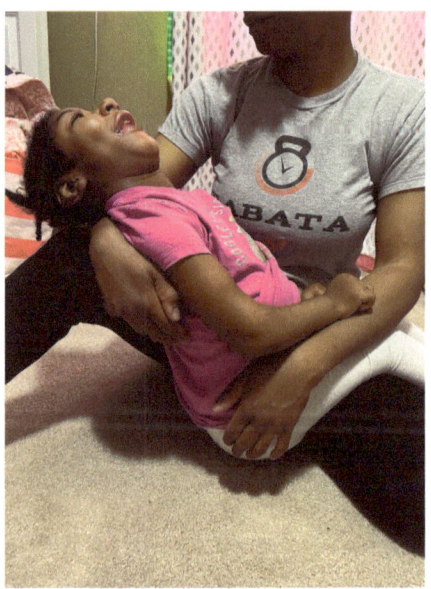

Prayer of Salvation and Surrender

Raising children with the direction of God can be challenging; imagine the challenges without His help and direction. If you have been touched by Marie's and our family's story and realize that you can no longer do life or parenting without Jesus, I encourage you to recite this prayer of salvation and surrender. I promise it's the first step to finding peace and freedom in parenting. Your life is about to change in amazing ways!

Prayer

"Father, I come before you humbly, surrendering my life and the burdens of my children to Your loving care. I first admit that I am a sinner and need your forgiveness. I believe that Jesus Christ died for my sins and rose again from the dead. I repent of my sins and ask for your forgiveness. I invite Jesus to come into my heart and be the Lord of my life. Thank you for your love and forgiveness.

As a parent, I recognize the limitations of my strength and wisdom in raising my children into what You want them to be.

Grant me the grace and courage to release my fears and anxieties, knowing that Your divine presence guides every step of our journey. Help me to relinquish control and embrace trust, knowing that You hold the ultimate plan for my life and the lives of our beloved children.

Guide me to let go of my personal aspirations for my life and my children's lives in exchange for Your desires. Give me the grace to make the necessary sacrifices to ensure my children fulfill their divine destiny.

In moments of doubt and uncertainty, may Your steadfast presence reassure me, illuminating the path ahead with Your unwavering light. Grant me the wisdom to discern Your will and the strength to follow it faithfully, even when the road ahead seems daunting.

May Your boundless love envelop my family, shielding us from harm and granting us the peace that surpasses all understanding. May Your grace transform our worries into prayers and our surrender into profound freedom in Your embrace.

As I surrender myself and my children into Your loving hands, may Your divine love reign rule in my heart, now and forevermore.

Amen."

Welcome to the family of God. As you continue on this journey, remember that His love and guidance are ever-present in your life and your children's lives. Trust in His plan, and may you find strength and peace in His reassuring presence every step of the way.

www.ingramcontent.com/pod-product-compliance
Lightning Source LLC
Chambersburg PA
CBHW041722070526
44585CB00001B/8